TIPS, TOOLS, & TECHNIQUES

To Care for Antiques, Collectibles, and Other Treasures

Georgia Kemp Caraway

NUMBER 5: PRACTICAL GUIDE SERIES

University of North Texas Press, Denton, Texas

10 9 8 7 6 5 4 3 2

Permissions:
University of North Texas Press
1155 Union Circle #311336
Denton, TX 76203-5017

The paper used in this book meets the minimum requirements of the American National Standard for Permanence of Paper for Printed Library Materials, z39.48.1984. Binding materials have been chosen for durability.

Library of Congress Cataloging-in-Publication Data

Caraway, Georgia Kemp, 1950–
  Tips, tools, and techniques to care for antiques, collectibles, and other treasures / Georgia Kemp Caraway.–1st ed.
    p. cm.—(Practical guide series ; no. 5)
  Includes bibliographical references.
  ISBN 978-1-57441-451-6 (pbk. : alk. paper)
  ISBN 978-1-57441-462-2 (e-book)
1. Collectibles—Conservation and restoration—Handbooks, manuals, etc. 2. Antiques—Conservation and restoration—Handbooks, manuals, etc. I. Title. II. Series: Practical guide series (Denton, Tex.) ; v. 5.
  NK1127.5.C36 2012
  745.028'8—dc23
                    2011048889

Tips, Tools, and Techniques to Care for Antiques, Collectibles, and Other Treasures is Number 5 in the Practical Guide Series

In memory of my husband
Bob Caraway
My antique lover for 32 years

CONTENTS

APPENDICES

PREFACE

TIPS FOR TAKING CARE OF YOUR ANTIQUES are not necessarily hard to find. What is hard to find is a practical list of tips with an easy-to-understand list of tools you may need to achieve this. That is the goal of this guide.

Many antiques are not just for display; collectors furnish their homes with these treasures and use them as part of their everyday lives. In fact, this book was compiled over several years because of my own need to care for and preserve my own antiques. It became even more crucial when I was charged as executive director of Denton County Museums with the care and preservation of artifacts in the Museums.

Although collectors are very good at collecting, and know that they must care for their collectibles, the practical knowledge for such care and attention was least understood due to the lack of some simple basic steps. The methods of care for historical or valuable antique items have changed over the years. No longer considered just functional, antique items should not be cared for or repaired in the same manner as modern home furnishings. While taking care of pieces can be very simple, the endeavor frequently causes damage or devalues the piece.

A WORD ABOUT ANTIQUE COLLECTING IS PERHAPS IN ORDER:

Antique collecting is the gathering of items of historical, aesthetic, and often monetary value from earlier times. The word *antique* applies legally and traditionally to an object that is more than 100 years old.

American collectors first concentrated on old books, manuscripts, the possessions and mementos of famous people, and classical antiquities. During the 20th century many sorts of objects in addition to paintings, books, and furniture attracted the collector's attention. Specialty collections grew of such items as jewelry, glass, coins, postage stamps, china, porcelain, silver, linens, bottles, stoneware, quilts, stamp boxes, scrimshaw, snuffboxes, fans, watches, clocks, postcards, photographs, periodicals, toys, folk art, military and political souvenirs, buttons, railroad, airline, and ship memorabilia, and advertising items.

Often the only value a popular object can claim is that of scarcity. Some items have become collector's items by virtue of their being nostalgic rather than having intrinsic value.

Markets are created by collectors and antique dealers of not only antiques but also objects that reflect characteristics of a particular style that is experiencing a revival of interest. These items may be sold or traded at antique shops, tag and rummage sales, garage sales, estate sales, auctions, antique shows, and flea markets. With the tremendous growth of interest in antiques, especially since the advent of the television program *Antiques Roadshow*, of necessity a critical expertise in historical styles and construction methods for the care and identification of precious objects has developed.

In 1909 the United States tariff regulations were altered to permit duty-free importation of antiques, defined as objects being more than 100 years old at the time of entry. More than 50 countries now have similar regulations.

As has been stated repeatedly on *Antiques Roadshow* and other antiques-related programs, you can destroy the monetary value of an antique by not taking the proper care of it.

If you are ever in doubt about how to care for an object, consult a professional before proceeding. And keep in mind the definitions for the care of antiques and collectibles:

- Cleaning simply means cleaning the piece
- Restoring means making repairs to the original condition
- Refinishing means stripping off the surface and redoing the finish of the piece
- Maintenance means to maintain the condition and value of the piece

And remember, collect what you love and lovingly take care of it!

Georgia
April 2012

Dr. Georgia Kemp Caraway is a passionate collector, teacher, and writer about antiques and collectibles. She has been teaching and writing about antiques and collectibles since 1988. She is executive director of the Texas Institute of Antiques & Collectibles in Denton, Texas, and was also the executive director of the Denton County Museums for thirteen years.

Georgia co-authored three Denton history books during her tenure as museum director. She writes a monthly column for the *Denton Record-Chronicle*, and has had articles on collecting and caring for antiques in the *Antique Almanac, Antique Prime*, and the *Latino Times* magazines. She was an appraiser for *Antiques Roadshow* and currently teaches courses on antiques and collectibles and owns enVogue & Vintage at the Antique Gallery in Denton, Texas. For more information on her classes, contact *georgiacaraway@aol.com*.

TOOLS TO KEEP ON HAND

- **Acid-free paper and boxes** (available from craft stores and library and museum suppliers). Protects photographs, prints, and textiles.
- **Black light.** A device that emits ultraviolet radiation (UV) light and can detect cracks in pottery and glue repairs in paper items.
- **Brushes.** Soft-bristled baby brushes (try saying that quickly!) are great for cleaning the delicate fabric on lampshades. Makeup brushes are great for cleaning Christmas ornaments and dusting delicate items with crevices.
- **Chalk.** Prevents silver from tarnishing.
- **Chamois.** Great for polishing mirrors and glassware, but the cloth will dry stiff as a board. To keep chamois soft, dry them quickly outside in the wind or in front of a fan, or in the dryer on air-dry. They will remain soft and pliable.
- **Covered telephone wire.** For mounting buttons onto display cards.

- **Crayons.** Use a color that matches the finish of the wood to hide scratches on furniture.
- **Twist ties.** Keep sets of cufflinks together.
- **Glare-free glass** (available from craft stores or frame shops). Protects photographs and prints from fading.
- **Monofilament.** Use as picture hanging wire for small, lighter-weight pictures.
- **Mothballs.** Place in silverware drawer or chest to prevent discoloration of silver.
- **Mounting corners** (clear). Use to mount photographs, trade cards, and advertising cards.
- **Pipecleaners.** Use with silver polish to clean between fork tines.
- **Q-Tips.** For cleaning any hard-to-reach crevices.
- **Socks.** Before moving a piece of heavy furniture, slip socks onto the legs. Also good protective storage covers for small breakables.
- **String.** Use with silver polish to clean between fork tines.
- **Superglue.** Repair glass and costume jewelry.
- **Toothbrushes** (soft). Use for any small hard-to-get-to crevices. Use with silver polish to remove tarnish from filigreed pieces or with furniture polish to remove dust on carved wood.
- **Toothpaste** (white paste). Cover a stain or scratch on acrylic or plastic with toothpaste. Let dry, then rub with soft cloth. Or as a quickie silver cleaner.
- **Toothpicks.** As a glue applicator.

Advertising Memorabilia: Metal

RESTORING METAL ADVERTISING MATERIALS

- If the paint has begun to peel or flake, do nothing. Any abrasive action will remove even more paint. Paint that is intact, but dirty, can be cleaned using soapy warm water and a soft cloth. Wrap the cloth around your index finger and apply only as much pressure as is necessary to loosen the dirt.

- Dull paint can be protected and the color enhanced with a coat of paste wax, but once again, be gentle for fear of damaging any loose paint.

Aluminum

REMOVING STAINS

- Place one to two cups of freshly cubed rhubarb in a stained aluminum pot. Add enough water to cover the stains. Stew over low heat until the stains are gone (usually less than an hour). Discard the cooked rhubarb. Wash and dry the pot. The acidity of the rhubarb will lift off stains.

SHINE AND BRIGHTEN

- To shine and brighten aluminum, use a silver polish such as Nevr-Dull.

REPAIRING HOLES

- Small holes in aluminum pieces that are not worth the expense of professional repair may be repaired at home. Hold a flat piece of iron inside and pound around the hole on the outside with a hammer. The aluminum is soft enough to expand and fill in a small hole. Do not attempt this on valuable collectible pieces.

OXIDATION

- Remove discoloration due to oxidation by filling a pan with a strong solution of vinegar and water.

OR

- Fill a pan with water and add two teaspoons of cream of tartar. Simmer for 15–20 minutes.

CLEANING

- Usually mild soap and warm water will do the trick. If a little stronger cleaning is needed, a gentle scrubbing with fine steel wool (0000) with a mild cleaner should work.

ALUMINUM CLEANER FORMULA

Use this only on hard to remove tarnish and greasy film on aluminum ware. Note that this may scratch and darken your piece. Do not use on collectible wares.

½ cup cream of tartar

½ cup baking soda

½ cup white vinegar

¼ cup soap flakes

Combine the cream of tartar and the baking soda in a medium-sized bowl. Add the vinegar and mix until the ingredients form a soft paste. Add the soap flakes and transfer to a jar or bottle with a secure lid. To use, apply gently with fine steel wool (0000). Rinse thoroughly. Label the jar and store out of the reach of children. Solution should keep one to two years.

AUDIO MATERIALS

The field of audio materials has been developing and changing over the last 134 years since Thomas A. Edison developed his phonograph and cylinders to convey the spoken word and music. Edison invented the first machine that could record sound in 1877 using a tinfoil cylinder. In 1886, Alexander Graham Bell obtained several patents for a commercial talking machine called a graphaphone. He replaced Edison's tinfoil with wax cylinders. By 1888, Edison had perfected his phonograph using a wax cylinder.

Some definitions of audio materials are in order. Audio records include 78s, 45s, and LPs (which are long-playing phonograph records designed to be played at 33 1/3 rpm). CD is a compact disc that is a plastic-fabricated, circular medium for recording, storing, and playing back audio, video, and computer data. DVDs used to be known as digital video discs until they became more versatile, thus the name change to digital versatile discs.

CLEANING AUDIO RECORDS, CDS, AND DVDS

- To clean really dirty or smudged records, CDs, or DVDs, use distilled water. It will not leave a residue on the disc.

Wipe the recording dry using a soft, nonabrasive, lint-free cloth.

- Dust audio records lightly by holding a soft cleaning brush as the record rotates on the player. Once the record has made several revolutions, remove the brush with a swift, light, perpendicular motion. Never touch the bristles of your record cleaning brush with your fingers as you will transfer oil and dirt to the brush.

- For more difficult dust on audio records, use the above method with a bit of distilled water or a few drops of record-cleaning solution. Be careful not to get the label wet. Be sure the surface of the record dries completely before you play or store it.

- Rub compact discs (CDs) gently from the center out with a soft, dry cloth. Never rub in circles as this could cause scratches that might render the disc unplayable.

- For more persistent smudges, try adding distilled water or CD cleaning solution and repeating above method. Be sure disc is dry before inserting into player.

HANDLING

- Do not touch the playing surfaces of any recordings. Clean your hands before handling recordings.

- Handle all grooved discs by their edge and label areas only. Handle compact discs by outer edge and center hole only.

- Handle open reel tapes by the outer edge of the reel flanges and center hub areas only. Do not squeeze flanges together—it will damage tape edges.

- Handle cassettes, audio and video tapes by outer shell, only. Do not place fingers or any other materials into openings.

- Handle wax cylinders by inserting middle and index fingers in the center hole, then gently spread them to just keep the cylinder from slipping off. Do not touch the grooves of wax cylinders; they are very susceptible to mold. Cylinders should be at room temperature before touching; the thermal shock from the warmth of your hand can cause cold wax cylinders to split.

STORAGE

- Keep all storage and use areas clean.

- Always store your recordings at a moderate temperature. Storage areas should be kept at a constant 65 to 70 degrees Fahrenheit and 45 to 50 percent relative humidity.

- Store in dark areas except when being accessed, being sure to keep recordings away from UV sources such as unfiltered fluorescent tubes and sunlight.

- Shelve all discs, open-reel and cassette tapes upright to reduce the tension on the media in its case or sleeve. Store cylinders standing on their ends. Do not lay any recording flat, not even audio or videocassettes.

- Generally demagnetization is not a problem. For an added margin of safety, to prevent demagnetization keep all open reel and cassette tapes away from potential sources of demagnetization, such as loudspeakers, most of which have sizable magnets in them. Do not set tapes on top of or leaning against any equipment which can be a source of either magnetic fields or heat. Be careful about operating machines with electric motors, such as vacuum cleaners, next to tape storage areas.

- Recordings are heavy and concentrate their weight in the center of a shelf, which can cause some shelving to collapse. Make sure that the shelving you choose is solid and well constructed.

- When possible, LPs and reel-to-reel tapes should be stored on metal shelves with the bottom shelf at least a few inches above the floor. If the recordings are stored on a wooden shelf or near the floor, remove immediately in case of a flood.

- Shelve discs vertically. Ideally, disc shelving should have full-height and full-depth dividers, spaced four to six inches apart, and secured at top and bottom. Less than full-height dividers may cause discs to warp. Interfiling discs of different diameter may also cause them to warp.

- Open reel tape boxes should be stored vertically. Dividers are not essential, but the boxes must be secured with a bookend and not allowed to fall.

- Audio and video cassette tapes in water repellent plastic containers should be stored vertically "on edge," not flat.

- Store cylinders standing "on end," like a drinking glass.

- Tapes should not be stored in the rewound or fast-forwarded position. Ideally, play a tape completely through, then store it without rewinding. Rewind it just before playing it again.

- As a general rule, it is usually best to store recordings in their original containers. However, some preservation experts suggest replacing the original record sleeve with a high-density polyethylene sleeve. In some cases the polyethylene sleeve can fit inside the original sleeve. If you use plastic sleeves, just be cautious of moisture build up.

- Collectors should keep all original materials pertaining to a recording in order to retain the value of the recorded material.

Bamboo Furniture

Bamboo is a fast-growing grass.

CLEANING

- Dust regularly with a vacuum or a dry cloth.
- To clean dust from hard-to-reach crevices of bamboo furniture, use a soft toothbrush or the brush attachment of a vacuum cleaner.
- Sponge dirty bamboo with a solution of warm water, mild detergent, and two to three teaspoons of ammonia. Rinse and wipe dry. Apply liquid wax occasionally.
- Shine bamboo with linseed or flax seed oil. Remove excess oil with a dry cloth.

PREVENTIVE CARE

- To prevent drying and splitting, take bamboo furniture outside once a year and wet with a fine spray from the garden hose. Or give it a quick shower in the bathroom. Let the piece dry slowly, out of the sun. If any bindings come loose, rewrap them and tack or glue into place.

Baskets

Baskets are made of organic material and should never become completely dry.

- One expert in basket collecting suggests sponging baskets with a solution of:

  40 percent castor oil

  60 percent alcohol

  Wipe off any excess solution with a soft cloth.

- Once a year, spritz your baskets with a fine spray of water and allow them to dry in a shady spot.

- Do not wet straw or rye baskets; they tend to mold.

Books

TEMPERATURE AND HUMIDITY CONTROL

- The ideal temperature range for storing books is 65 to 75 degrees Fahrenheit, with 50 percent relative humidity.
- Direct sunlight, artificial light, or intense heat can dry out and fade leather and cloth bindings.
- Avoid displaying or storing books near heat sources.

WATER SPILLS AND FLOODING

- A frost-free freezer will draw out the moisture and free the pages that have stuck together. If water has damaged too many books to fit in the freezer, call a local wholesale meat distributor or food processor and arrange to rent freezer space.

CLEANING

- Clean leather bindings with saddle soap, neat's foot oil, castor oil, or white petroleum jelly. Apply sparingly with your fingers, a piece of felt, cheesecloth, or a chamois. Wait several hours, and then repeat.
- Use an art gum or soap eraser to clean dingy hardbound book covers and page ends. While cleaning, be sure to hold the book tightly closed to prevent damaging the pages.

- Clean books with a vacuum dusting-brush attachment, a shaving brush, or a soft paintbrush. Dust from the back binding to the front, not allowing dust to gather in the headcap.
- Check books periodically for insect infestation. Bookworms, moths, and silverfish love to chew on pages and bindings. Remove any insect carcasses with a soft brush.
- Wipe mold and mildew off the bindings and pages with a clean soft cloth. If the pages are still moldy, wipe with an alcohol-dampened cloth, then fan out the pages and brush off after a few hours.
- Use a dry chemical sponge available from janitorial supply stores to clean soot from fire damage.
- Press a lump of untinted modeling clay over the dirt on soiled pages. Knead the clay frequently to get a fresh surface.

DISPLAY

- When arranging books on shelves, be sure there is plenty of room for each one to be lifted out easily.
- Books should be held upright on shelves.
- Use bookends on partially filled shelves so that books stand upright. Prevent books from sagging and spines from bending.
- Keep books away from the back of the bookcase to allow for air circulation.
- Paper and clothbound books should not be stored or displayed next to leather bound books. Acidity and oils from the leather may migrate into paper and cloth.

- Never place newspaper clippings between book pages because this will cause discoloration and paper deterioration.
- If books are rare, line your bookshelves with acid-free paper or use glass shelves. Be careful of weight load if using glass shelves.
- Protect books with polypropylene or milex covers.

REPAIRING BROKEN BOOKS

- Broken signatures can be resewn carefully, using heavy cotton thread. Do not use polyester thread, which can cut through the paper. Make sure you sew through the original holes as closely as possible.

TORN PAGES

- Glue rice paper or onionskin over the tears or mend with gummed tissue. Sandwich newly repaired pages between sheets of wax paper so that they will not stick to other pages.

DOG-EARED CORNERS

- Put a sheet of paper on top of the creased paper and press with a warm iron.

STORAGE

- Never store reading materials in a damp place such as a basement or garage. Moisture leads to rotten leather bindings, sticky glossy-stock pages, and foxing (yellowish-brown stains that mar the pages).

LOANING BOOKS (NEITHER A BORROWER OR A LENDER BE, BUT IF YOU MUST ...)

- Put your name inside your loaned book in *pencil*. Keep a 3 x 5 card with the name of the book, the borrower's name, and the date loaned. Or keep the dust jacket and pencil the borrower's name inside as a reminder.

BRASS

Brass is an alloy of copper and zinc. Two parts of copper are usually used to one part zinc.

CLEANING LACQUERED BRASS

- Lacquer coating on brass preserves the shine and prevents oxidation or tarnishing. Clean with a mild detergent and water, then rinse and wipe dry. Avoid harsh abrasives that can wear through the lacquer.

REMOVING LACQUER FROM NEW BRASS

- Manufacturers of new brass fixtures coat the metal with a lacquer varnish to preserve its shine. To remedy this, you can soak new brass for a few minutes in acetone (the basis for nail polish remover, available at most hardware stores). Wearing gloves, scrub with a soft scouring pad and rinse. Work in a well-ventilated area, and keep acetone covered. Exposed to air, the brass will begin to oxidize, darkening noticeably in a few months.

AGING NEW BRASS SCREWS

- Put screws in lacquer thinner overnight to remove the coating. Scuff with fine steel wool (0000). Rub screws in the palm of your hand. Your natural oils will start tarnishing the screws immediately. Screws will continue to tarnish after you have installed them.

UNLACQUERED BRASS CLEANING FORMULA

This formula is tough enough for black cooked-on grease and food.

- ½ cup all-purpose flour
- ½ cup salt
- ½ cup powdered detergent
- ¾ cup white vinegar
- ¼ cup lemon juice
- ½ cup very warm water

In a large glass bowl, mix the flour, salt, and detergent well. Pour in the remaining ingredients and stir. Transfer the mixture to a glass quart jar, close tightly, and label. Store out of reach of children.

To use, test first on an inconspicuous area. Shake briskly, then pour some of the cleaner on cookware and rub gently with a cloth. For tough spots, scrub with an old toothbrush or a plastic scouring pad. Rinse with clear water, dry, and polish with a soft cloth.

TECHNIQUES FOR CLEANING
UNLACQUERED BRASS

- Submerge overnight in equal parts water and ammonia. Rub with extra fine steel wool (0000) or a soft brush. Rinse and dry item and seal with paste wax.

  Or

- Scrub lightly with a soft brush dampened with a little ammonia. Rinse and dry item and seal with paste wax.

  Or

- Rub with regular or gel toothpaste. Rinse and dry item and seal with paste wax.

  Or

- Pour tomato ketchup on item. Rinse and dry item and seal with paste wax.

  Or

- Use Worcestershire sauce. Rinse and dry item and seal with paste wax.

  Or

- Soak in water in which onions have been boiled. Rinse and dry item and seal with paste wax.

  Or

- Use a lemon juice and salt paste. Rinse and dry item and seal with paste wax.

  Or

- Soak item in vinegar. Moisten rag with vinegar, dip in salt and rub item. Rinse with vinegar. Rinse and dry item and seal with paste wax.

  Or

- Dip lemon slice in salt and rub slice over the item. Rinse with vinegar. Rinse and dry item and seal with paste wax.

OR

- Use two parts vinegar, one part lemon juice. Soak item. Rinse and dry item and seal with paste wax.

NONTOXIC FORMULA FOR CLEANING BRASS

    2   teaspoons salt

    2   teaspoons flour

    2   teaspoons vinegar

Mix ingredients together to form a paste. Apply to the brass and let mixture dry. Wash with warm, sudsy water. Rinse thoroughly and buff dry.

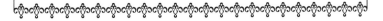

NONTOXIC FORMULA FOR CLEANING BRASS

    2   tablespoons pulverized limestone powder (also called rottenstone; available at hardware stores)

      small amount of vegetable or olive oil

      few drops of vinegar

Make a paste of the above ingredients. Rub until the metal looks bright. Wash and polish dry.

Bronze

Bronze is an alloy of copper and tin.

- Solid bronze is often given a coating of clear lacquer at the factory to protect the finish. Lacquered bronze needs only dusting and occasional wiping with a damp cloth. If the lacquer cracks or peels, have it refinished.
- Unlacquered bronze can be washed, if required, with mild soap or detergent and water. Hot vinegar or hot buttermilk has also been suggested. Rinse and wipe dry with a clean, soft cloth.
- To brighten bronze, rub it with polish specifically made for bronze.

BUTTONS

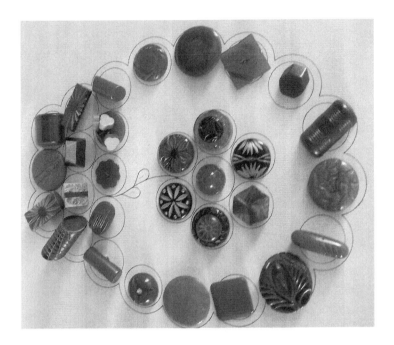

Buttons are made of practically every material known to man. Use these tips to apply to other items made of the same materials.

- Avoid storing buttons of different materials together. Also, do not store buttons in deteriorating or dirty condition. Clean them first using the following methods.
- Black rubber buttons should not be washed in water. Use Kiwi Cavalier Heel and Shoe Dressing, a good furniture polish, or baby oil to restore and shine.

- Brass buttons will turn green when the brass plating has worn off. Copper also becomes covered with green copper carbonate due to exposure to moisture in the air. Remove the green by rubbing the button gently with acetic acid or any substance containing this acid (such as vinegar). Wash the button with fresh water and dry well with a hairdryer or an absorbent towel. Do not store until completely dry. If the buttons are pierced, be sure that the inside of the button is dry. This is when a hairdryer comes in handy. Gel or regular toothpaste also works, but do not use on pierced buttons. It is too difficult to remove the paste completely from the crevices.

- Composite buttons are made of multiple types of materials, such as pearl on brass, metal on plastic, or celluloid on Bakelite. Clean each material using the individual instructions for that material. Use caution when dealing with varied construction.

- Composition buttons are made of a mixture of substances. Polish with baby oil, mineral oil, furniture polish, or Johnson's Neutral Self Shining Shoe Polish.

- China and ceramic buttons (when the design is fired on or fused into the button) can be cleaned with warm soapy water, a damp cloth, or glass cleaner. If there is any chance that the design may rub off, do not clean.

- Clean enamel buttons by using a toothbrush dipped in ammonia. This will remove all traces of dirt and grease from the surface of the enamel. It also brightens any gilded metal surface. If large areas of the metal have become corroded, rub with fine grade steel wool (0000) moistened with a bit of sewing machine oil to remove the discoloration. Caution: if the button has painted surfaces combined with the enamel, the ammonia will remove the painted surfaces, but will not harm the enamel.

- Clean fabric buttons by immersing them in a jar of dry-cleaning fluid and shaking gently. Remove and dry thoroughly on an absorbent towel. Some fabric buttons may withstand washing in warm soapy water.

  - It is best to remove dust from *passementerie* buttons with a soft brush. Spot clean with dry-cleaning fluid on a Q-Tip.
  - Thread-back fabric buttons should be handled very carefully as some of the threads that compose the shank may be brittle and break easily.
  - Glued trim on fabric buttons should be cleaned with cloth dampened with dry-cleaning fluid. Particular care should be taken if the trim is a different material than fabric.
  - Black cloth buttons may be freshened by applying black ink with a brush.

- Glass buttons should be carefully studied before cleaning to be sure that paint, paper backs, and other fragile construction will not be destroyed by immersion in water.

  - Fragile glass buttons (painted backs, kaleidoscopes, paper backs, and watch crystals) should be cleaned very carefully with a Q-Tip dipped in soapy water and dried thoroughly.
  - Other types of glass buttons can be put safely in a pan of warm water with liquid soap (not powdered

or dishwasher soap). Soak for a short time. Brush with a soft toothbrush. Rinse in water and dry thoroughly with a soft cloth.

- Glass buttons set in metal should not be immersed in water. Treat as you would a fragile button, by wiping the glass surface with a damp cloth or Q-Tip. Shine the metal with a pencil eraser or with fine grade steel wool (0000).

• Horn buttons become dry and need to have their natural oils restored from time to time. Rub a bit of lanolin, baby oil, or mineral oil onto the surface of the button. Let stand for a few minutes. Rub with a soft cloth to remove any excess oil.

- When black dye has worn off the surface of horn buttons, apply a bit of black shoe polish to the surface. Rub with a soft cloth. Use a shoe brush to remove any excess polish.
- To protect horn buttons from infestation of moth larvae and termites, store them in an enclosed carton or plastic envelope with a few mothballs.
- Natural horn buttons can be made to look better by using Kiwi Leather Balm or any natural cream shoe polish. Rub the backs of the buttons with Lysol or furniture oil for a protective coating.

• Ivory or bone buttons can yellow with use and age. To restore, cut a lemon in half, dip it in salt and rub over the surface. Allow buttons to dry. Wipe with a damp cloth and buff dry. Baby oil can be used on ivory buttons to revive their sheen.

- Brighten leather buttons by using saddle soap or a neutral shoe cream. Also baby oil or mineral oil may be used. Neat's foot oil will protect leather buttons from drying out, but will not add shine.

- Metal buttons can be polished with a polishing cloth to remove tarnish and brighten the surface. Metal polish can be used, but use a soft toothbrush to be sure that all the polish is removed from the crevices. Sometimes using a pencil eraser will clean and shine the surface. (This is one of my favorite nontoxic methods).

- Pearl or iridescent shell is a natural, somewhat porous substance. Avoid putting buttons in a soap and water bath. Spray them with WD-40 and let soak for a few hours. This will loosen the dirt covering or chalky layer found on the buttons. Wipe clean and use fine grade steel wool (0000) to buff the buttons. Polish with MAAS or use a similar metal paste polish. Use a toothpick to remove any chalky residue remaining in any crevices of carved buttons.

  - Bring back the luster to pearl and shell buttons by gently rubbing the button with baby oil or mineral oil on a soft cloth. If the button is painted or is engraved pearl with paint-filled lines, carefully go over the surface with a soft cloth.

- Pewter can be cleaned with any of the metal polishes such as Brasso, Wenol, or MAAS. For stubborn spots, use an eraser or Turtle Wax Chrome Polish.

  - The least expensive way to polish pewter is to use the outer leaves of cabbage. After rubbing the leaves over the surface, buff with a soft cloth. You will be astonished at the result.

- Plastic or celluloid buttons should never be stored with metal buttons. Certain plastics will corrode metal buttons because of their chemical makeup. Nor should celluloid buttons be stored in metal containers.

  - Use MAAS to clean celluloid surfaces. Never submerge celluloid buttons in water. If there is metal under the celluloid, it will rust from underneath and ruin the celluloid.

- Scrimshaw buttons made with polyester should only be dusted. Washing could remove the ink or cause the ink to run.

- Silver buttons should be cleaned with silver polish or cotton wadding such as Nevr Dull. Be sure that all the polish is removed from the surface of the button by washing and rubbing with a soft cloth. Do not use liquid silver polish on reticulated silver buttons.

  - An inexpensive homemade silver polish is a paste of three parts baking soda to one part water. Rub, wash, and polish with a soft cloth.

- Steel or cut-steel buttons are treated differently from other metal buttons. The simplest way to remove rust on these buttons is with lead from a pencil. After rubbing the lead over the surface, use a soft cloth to rub the button and a toothbrush to remove all traces of the lead graphite. To inhibit future rusting, spray with WD-40 and polish with any good metal polish.

- Remove rust from button shanks by using fine steel wool (0000). A magnet can be used to remove the residue.

- If the steel has a blue tint, it is better to leave the rust alone unless most of the tint is gone and you want to remove the remainder.

- Naval jelly can be used if a button is badly rusted, but it is highly corrosive and must be removed immediately. Use caution and wear protective rubber gloves.

- Small patches of rust may clean up with a typewriter eraser. The eraser will remove the spots and will not scratch the surface of the button.

• Tin and zinc buttons can be cleaned with the soft eraser on a lead pencil. If the button is badly corroded, use a metal polish sprinkled on a soft cloth. Baking soda or a commercial product such as Soft Scrub or Barkeepers Friend will give good results.

• Restore Vegetable Ivory buttons by applying baby oil or furniture polish, Kiwi Leather Balm may also be used.

• Wooden buttons may be cleaned with furniture polish or baby oil.

• Do not use pipe cleaners for mounting buttons. The metal interior can rust and corrode the buttons. Plastic-coated telephone wire or plastic-coated twist ties are the best holders for mounting buttons on display cards.

Cast Iron

Cast iron is an alloy of iron containing so much carbon that it is brittle and so cannot be wrought but must be shaped by casting.

Cast iron retains heat well, making it a popular choice for cooks, but it can be difficult to keep clean and sanitary.

SEASONING CAST IRON COOKWARE

- To season a new cast iron skillet or griddle (or one that has been scoured), rub lightly with vegetable shortening. Coat both the exterior and the interior. Heat the utensil in a 250-degree oven for two hours. Vegetable oil is not recommended. It tends to leave a sticky coating.
- The first few times you use cast iron utensils, cook foods high in fat, such as fried chicken or bacon, to build up the seasoning.
- Wash cast iron after it has cooled with a little dishwashing liquid. According to the experts, detergents will not remove the seasoning. Do not soak the cookware.
- If any food has stuck to the surface, use a scouring pad, then rub shortening over the area. Always be sure to oven dry or air-dry your cast iron completely to avoid rust. Store uncovered.

- Never store food in cast iron cookware. The surface is porous and will absorb odors and flavors.

CLEANING ENAMELED CAST IRON

- Clean with a soft pad or natural bristle brush. If food is stuck to the pan, it can be left to soak and then gently scrubbed with a nylon sponge. Never use steel wool or abrasives on enameled cookware.

CEDAR AROMA RENEWAL

Cedar's distinctive aroma comes from exposed fibers in the wood.

RENEWING THE SCENT OF CEDAR

- To renew the scent inside a piece of furniture (or a closet) it is necessary to go over the surface with fine sandpaper to expose a new layer of fibers. Use a filter mask as protection against the dust created by sanding.

   After sanding the cedar, be sure to leave the wood untreated, as any finish will retard the fresh scent. If the piece of furniture was previously stained or painted, remove the old finish before sanding.

CHINA

China is used interchangeably with *porcelain* to describe white, hard, permanent, nonporous ceramic ware having translucence, and which is resonant when struck. *China* is a shortened version of *chinaware* and *china dishes.*

REMOVING BROWN SPOTS FROM CHINA

- You may successfully remove brown spots caused by water and dirt under the glaze of china. If you are not sure of yourself, consult a professional restorer.

- This method of cleaning collectible china (Flow Blue, Ironstone, Harker Cameo, etc.) has been tested by experts and proven effective. This method will remove brown spots and lighten the effects from crazing.

Clear hydrogen peroxide, 30 or 40 percent volume, may be safely used to clean your china pieces. This solution can be obtained at your local beauty supply dealer. If they do not stock clear hydrogen peroxide in these percentages, ask them to order it. Never use hydrogen peroxide over 40 percent. It is too strong.

Work in a well-ventilated area, and do not breathe the fumes. Do not expose your skin or eyes to the peroxide. Wear rubber gloves, as the hydrogen peroxide can burn your skin.

Pour the peroxide into an airtight, plastic container that has a sealable cover. Hydrogen peroxide is combustible. Do not place the container near a heater or an open flame.

Submerge your china in the solution and seal the cover. Check the container every few days by carefully opening the lid. You will notice that the discoloration has begun to disappear. Very dirty pieces may take one and a half weeks of soaking.

Protect your hands with rubber gloves and take the pieces out of the hydrogen peroxide solution. Wash them in soapy water, and then place them in the sun to dry.

If discoloration is still unacceptable, you may place the pieces in an *electric* oven set no higher than 150 degrees to pull discoloration through the crazing to the surface. Use aluminum foil to protect your oven from secretions. The heat process should be done very carefully so as not to add to the crazing. NEVER USE A GAS OVEN. After 30 minutes in the oven, allow the china to cool before rinsing the residue off. Place china back in the hydrogen peroxide and repeat all the steps until no discoloration surfaces during the heat process.

EFFECT OF BLEACH ON CHINA

Do not use bleach on china or pottery to remove stains. Bleach leaves an oily residue and makes the china heavier and dead feeling. Bleach will penetrate the glaze causing it to start flaking off. The bleach will also continue to surface through the crazing and appear dusty and dull.

- If you have a piece of china that you suspect has been bleached, you can neutralize it in a mixture of half white distilled vinegar and half water. In most cases, this will help stop the action of the bleach.

REMOVING STAINS FROM CHINA CUPS

- Scrub cups with a paste of baking soda and water.
  Or
- Scrub with a 50-50 mixture of salt and white vinegar.
  Or
- Place in denture-cleaning solution and soak overnight.
  Or
- For a brilliant shine, rinse fine china in half-cup borax in a sink of warm water. Rinse again in clear water.

MENDING BROKEN SOFT PASTE POTTERY USING ELMER'S GLUE

- Wash the surface of the piece. Put glue on a Q-Tip and apply a thin coating to each surface. Fit the pieces together. Clean the face and underside of the piece with water to remove excess glue. Use masking tape to hold firmly in place until the glue dries. Leave a tab of tape for easy removal. One expert suggests putting the piece in a box of sand to hold it steady. Allow the piece to dry at least five hours before washing or using it.

Christmas Ornaments

- Do not wash vintage Christmas ornaments. The lacquer is water-soluble.
- Use a soft makeup brush to dust ornaments. Anything stiffer, even tissue paper, will lift off the lacquer.
- Do not store ornaments in the basement or attic. Moisture and temperature changes can cause irreparable harm to delicate decorations. Glass or enamel can crack; paper and cardboard can become brittle and crumble. Moisture can cause mold or mildew and attract silverfish that eat glue and paper.
- Store ornaments wrapped in acid-free tissue inside acid-free cardboard boxes. The best method is to store ornaments in acid-free boxes with compartments so that ornaments do not touch each other. Store the boxes under a bed or in another air-conditioned location. Do not store in plastic boxes that will trap moisture.
- Do not fold paper goods or fabrics. Laying paper flat in boxes and rolling textiles wrapped in cotton or muslin is ideal.
- Do not expose vintage ornaments to sunlight.
- Be sure to check the caps of the ornaments before hanging them on the tree. If they are not secure, the caps can spring off easily.

CHROME

Chrome is a compound or alloy of chromium.

- Wipe with a soft, damp cloth and polish with a dry cloth.
- If sticky, wash with a mild soap or detergent. A little kerosene on a damp cloth, or baking soda on a dry cloth, is excellent for sticky surfaces.
- MAAS is very good for polishing chrome and for removing small surface scratches.

COINS

Only trust experts to clean collectible and valuable coins. The slightest damage can devalue their numismatic value.

- That said, if you still want to clean your coins, first try a general light soaking in mild soapy water (liquid soap, not dishwasher detergent).

If this does not do the job, the following solution is offered:

COIN CLEANING FORMULA

> 2 small drinking glasses (one for copper, one for silver coins)
>
> 1 coffee can for rinsing
>
> 1 teaspoon table salt
>
> 2 tablespoons white vinegar

Make two solutions if you are cleaning both copper and silver coins. Using the same solution for both often turns your silver coins pink or copper colored.

Pour salt and vinegar into each glass. This amount of solution will clean six to eight coins at a time. Some coins will be cleaned in a matter of seconds, so do not clean more coins than you can handle. The coins will turn dull if left in the solution too long.

CONTINUED

Fill the rinse can with cold water and leave the can under a slow running tap. As the coins show brightly in the solution, remove them and drop them into the rinse water. Some coins will be stubborn and difficult to clean. Help them along by rubbing them with your fingers then drop them back into the mix. Most will come clean in seconds or minutes.

After rinsing the coins for about three minutes, wipe them or spread them out on a paper towel to dry.

It is easy to damage your coins permanently unless great care is taken in keeping the cleaning solution separated for the different types of coins. Nickels, pennies, and silver coins should be cleaned each in their own bath. Otherwise, nickels when cleaned in a penny solution will turn red.

USING ELECTROLYSIS

Electrolysis is another way to clean coins, but it works by removing a tiny portion of the coin's surface. Electrolysis cleaners are generally used on very badly corroded coins.

Follow the instructions carefully when using electrolysis cleaners. These cleaners work by sending a small current through the coin while it is submerged in a solution of water and citric acid. The higher the current, the faster the surface metal will be removed from the coins. The surface corrosion breaks up as metal is removed from the coins. Coins are usually left in the bath from one to ten minutes. Following the electrolysis bath the coins must be scrubbed with a small, soft brush and dried thoroughly.

COLORFAST FABRICS

The secret to making fabric, floss, yarns, and threads color-fast is white vinegar.

- For small items use a plastic container. For larger items, use a large sink or a bathtub. Mix one part white vinegar with one part water in the container. After immersing the item, examine the solution. If the water begins to take on the fabric color, immediately flush the item with very cold water.

Make a new solution using very cold water. Soak the item for at least 30 minutes occasionally agitating the container. Be sure that all parts of the item are well saturated.

Take the item out and lay it on a terry cloth towel. Roll the towel, squeezing gently. Do not wring or twist the water out of the item.

Very gently shape the item for drying. Air dry out of direct sunlight.

COPPER

Copper is a nonferrous mineral with very high thermal and electrical conductivity.

COPPER POLISH NONTOXIC FORMULA

   2 tablespoons pulverized limestone powder (also called rottenstone; available at hardware stores)

      small amount of vegetable or olive oil

      few drops of vinegar

Make a paste of the above ingredients. Rub until the metal looks bright. Wash and polish dry.

OTHER COPPER POLISH METHODS

- Pour hot white vinegar and salt solution over copper and rub. Rinse immediately and dry.

  OR

- Wipe buttermilk onto copper with soft cloth. Rinse and dry.

Or

• Dip half a lemon in table salt and rub on the item. Let the item stand a few minutes, then rinse in warm, sudsy water.

Or

• Dip slice or wedge of lemon in baking soda. Rub, rinse, and dry.

COPPER CLEANING NONTOXIC FORMULA

    2 teaspoons salt

    2 teaspoons flour

    2 teaspoons vinegar

Mix ingredients together to form a paste. Apply to the piece and let the mix dry. Wash with warm, sudsy water. Rinse thoroughly and buff dry.

COPPER CLEANING FORMULA

This formula is tough enough for black, cooked-on grease and food.

    ½ cup all-purpose flour

    ½ cup salt

    ½ cup powdered laundry detergent

CONTINUED

¾ cup white vinegar

¼ cup lemon juice

½ cup very warm water

Mix the flour, salt, and detergent well in a large glass bowl. Pour in the remaining ingredients and stir. Transfer the mixture to a glass quart jar, close tightly, and label. Store out of reach of children.

To use, shake briskly, then pour some of the cleaner on cookware and rub gently with a dishcloth. For tough spots, scrub with a soft toothbrush, or a plastic scouring pad (test first on an inconspicuous area to be sure that you are not scratching the surface). Rinse with clear water, dry, and polish with a soft cloth.

REMOVING PROTECTIVE LACQUER FROM COPPER

• Mix ¼ cup baking soda per gallon of water and bring to a boil. Place the copperware in the boiling water bath and continue to boil for 15 minutes or more. Remove the copper piece. The coating should peel off easily. Wash and dry thoroughly. The pan is ready for use.

"GREEN MOLD" ON COPPER

• Mix equal parts of ketchup and mayonnaise. Dab on copper area affected by the green mold. Leave solution on for a few minutes. Wash off and dry. Do not try this with jewelry that has green mold around real or fake pearls.

Dolls

If your doll is badly damaged, has missing parts, or extremities that have come unstrung, consult with a doll restoration expert. For simple refurbishing, do the following:

CLEANING DOLL CLOTHES

- Test a small part of the clothing in cold water to be sure the fabric is colorfast. If not, follow the colorfast instructions in this book (see page 38).

Gently wash garment in a mild detergent.

Add a tablet of Efferdent to 1½ cups of hot water in a large, open plastic container Allow to cool slightly. Place laundered garment in the solution.

Gently agitate with a wooden spoon. Soak for 15 minutes. Rinse with tepid water and equal parts of white vinegar. Soak for three to five minutes. The vinegar will neutralize the chlorine in the Efferdent. Roll garment loosely in a towel. Gently reshape garment and dry away from sunlight and heat.

For various problem stains, follow some of the stain removal tips located under the Fabric and Textiles section of this book. Use caution when dealing with doll clothes, because the little girls who played with them probably did not handle the clothes too gently.

IRONING DOLL CLOTHES

- Use the lowest temperature possible that will still produce steam. Cover the garment with a thin pressing cloth. Test a small area before your start. Work slowly. Be sure garment is dry and cool before you handle it.
- When pressing very small garments, use a curling iron wrapped in a thin pressing cloth.

CLEANING DIRT FROM PORCELAIN, RUBBER, AND COMPOSITION DOLLS

- Use caution and test a small inconspicuous part of the doll before attempting to clean.
- For smudges and dirt, gently rub with a pencil eraser.

- For ink stains, spray hairspray on a Q-Tip and rub gently over the affected area.
- Where Barbie's earrings have stained her ears and face with green mold, use Oxy-10 on a Q-Tip.
- For eye crazing in composition dolls, put a drop of sewing machine oil on the eye.
- To enrich the body surface of a composition doll, rub on a small amount of Pond's Cold Crème.

STORING DOLLS

- Do not store dolls in an attic, garage, barn, or shed or any place where seasonal temperature changes occur. Dolls should be stored at room temperature in a place with normal humidity.
- Dolls should be kept dust free.
- Dolls with wigs of human hair, mohair, wool, fur, or yarn should not be stored without mothballs or similar moth and bug preventative.
- Do not store dolls in plastic bags. Condensation can build up and the dolls will not be able to breathe.
- Dolls with movable eyes should be stored face down. This will keep the eyes open and prevent them from sticking closed. It will also prevent the eyes from falling to the back of the head and potentially cracking the china head.
- Dolls with china or bisque feet or lower legs should have a spool placed between them with a string through the spool and tied around each ankle. This will prevent the legs from clacking together.

DOORSTOPS

- A doorstop with good original paint can be cleaned using cotton swabs and a mild furniture spray wax. This cleans, leaves a light wax, and brings out the color.
- Use a soft toothbrush with lukewarm water and mild soap if the doorstop is dirty.
- Sometimes a mild abrasive cleaner diluted with water may be needed. Extreme caution is recommended to avoid removing the original paint. Some colors come off easily. Test a minor part of the doorstop before using abrasives. After the piece is completely dry, a light coat of wax will bring out the color.
- Do not remove surface layers of paint on overpainted pieces unless you are experienced at paint restoration. It is very easy to remove the original paint while removing the overpainted surface.

ENAMEL

Enamel is an opaque or semitransparent glassy substance applied to metallic or other hard surfaces for ornament or as a protective coating.

- Boil peeled potatoes in enamel cookware to remove stains.

  Or

- Clean white enamel by rubbing the surface with turpentine.

  Or

- Rub surface with baking soda.

  Or

- For stubborn stains, soak in sodium hypochlorite solution and wash with soap and water. Sodium hypochlorite can be found in hardware stores.

Fabrics and Textiles

See the section on Upholstery, Rugs, and Carpet Cleaning for tips on fabric used on furniture. Also see Vintage Clothing and Textiles for information about especially delicate items.

Before taking steps yourself to preserve and care for antique fabrics, you should seek professional advice about specific conservation, cleaning, storage, and exhibition problems. Each fabric is unique and requires individual consideration. With that warning in mind, follow these general rules for fabric care.

CARE OF OLD FABRICS

- **Provide a stable environment for the textile.** Protect it from rough handling, light, extreme changes of temperature and humidity, and insects. For each of these problems there is a simple remedy.

- **Handling.** When you must handle fabrics, clean your hands first. Remove sharp jewelry to prevent snags and tears. Do not eat, drink, or smoke near the article. Keep article away from unclean surfaces, and do not place any objects on top of it.

- **Light.** Light is harmful to textiles. Many older fabrics are made of cellulose (cotton and linen) and animal (wool and silk) fibers. These are damaged by ultraviolet rays of the sun and fluorescent light, and by the heat of incandescent light.

Reduce the light that falls upon your textiles. Keep your draperies drawn when possible. Do not place lamps near textiles. Use ultraviolet filters on windows and lamps.

- **Climate control.** Try to maintain a room temperature of 70 degrees Fahrenheit and a relative humidity of 50 percent where you have vintage fabrics stored. These are the best conditions for preserving fabrics. Control the environment with humidifiers, dehumidifiers, air conditioners, and heating units.

  Do not store textiles in basements or attics. Prevent excessive dryness and eliminate dampness that could foster mold and mildew.

  If a textile is already damp, fast drying is important to inhibit mold growth. Fans and electric heaters can help.

- **Insects and rodents.** Frequent vacuuming and cleaning of storage areas and regular inspection, rotation, and airing of textiles will help keep these critters away. Consult a professional when it is necessary to use chemicals to kill these creatures.

STAIN REMOVAL FROM FABRICS

Stains should be removed before washing items. "Do it now" should be the rule when a stain occurs. Consult a conservator before attempting to treat stains on fragile or valuable fabrics or textiles. But if you wish to try some home remedies that work well, use the following tips.

- **Berries.** Treat a wet stain by sprinkling the area with salt. Rub area with damp soap. Allow mixture to remain on textile for a few hours. Rinse well. For dried stains, soak the item in a solution of one part borax and six parts water. For sturdy fabrics, pour boiling water through the stain until the spot disappears.

- **Blood.**   Soak the item in cold water then wash with mild soap and tepid water. Stubborn stains may be removed, from cotton only, by soaking in a solution of sodium hypochlorite.

  Or

  Put a paste of water and cornstarch, cornmeal, or talcum powder on fresh spots. Let dry and brush off.

  Or

  Cover fresh or dried blood with meat tenderizer and add cool water. After 15 to 30 minutes, sponge off with cool water.

- **Fresh blood on leather.**   Dab on a little hydrogen peroxide. After it bubbles, wipe it off.

- **Fresh blood on fabric.** If you prick your finger while sewing and get blood on the fabric, quickly wet a long piece of white cotton thread with saliva and place it on the spot. The thread will absorb the blood.

- **Brown Spots.** Use commercial products, such as Lily-White Linens, Orvus, or Oxyclean.

  Or

  Treat the area with hot juice made from cooked rhubarb stems. (See Rust formula). Repeat the application as needed.

- **Chocolate or Cocoa.** Blot up or scrape off excess chocolate. Apply a solution of ½ teaspoon mild detergent in one pint of water. Blot with clean white towel. If the stain remains, apply a solution of one tablespoon of ammonia in one cup of water. Again blot with clean white towel. If the stain still remains, use a fifty-fifty solution of white vinegar and water. Then blot again.

- **Coffee or Tea.** If you are able to treat the stain immediately, apply a solution of one part borax and six parts water. Wash the item in warm, soapy water using a gentle cleanser such as Orvus or Lily-White Linens. If the stain has already dried, loosen it with an application of one part glyceride to one part water.

  OR

  To remove stubborn stains on sturdy fabrics, try hot water, then bleach. Or moisten stain with lemon juice and expose item to the sun. If colors are apt to run, use only tepid water, followed by mild soap and weak ammonia. Hydrogen peroxide is a stronger bleach for woolens and silks.

- **Cream and Milk.** Soak article in hot water then launder with mild soap and warm water.

- **Eggs.** Soak linens or cottons in cold water. Rub silk with table salt. Launder.

- **Fruits.** Lemon and citrus fruit juices should be sponged with clear water and then with a weak solution of ammonia. Treat other fruit juice stains as you would coffee stains.

- **Grass.** Soak the stain well with kerosene then brush out with gasoline or alcohol. Use caution! These liquids are flammable.

- **Grease and oils.** Lay item over blotting paper and sponge with gasoline or benzene. Benzene and gasoline are highly flammable and should not be stored in large amounts in the home.

- **Ink.** Ink stains are very difficult remove.

  - Ballpoint ink. Test an inconspicuous part of the fabric with hair spray or nail polish remover. If no damage is done, blot the ink spot with a cloth dampened with the solvent and then with a dry cloth. For white cotton fabrics, apply petroleum jelly; rub gently in a detergent solution. As a last resort, use chlorine bleach on bleachable items.

  - Felt tip markers. Place the stained area over an absorbent towel and sponge with another cloth dampened with cleaning fluid. Then place the fabric in sunlight, which will lighten the stain further.

  - A 1937 almanac suggests cold water, or turpentine, alcohol, ammonia, or weak oxalic acid over an absorbent towel.

- **Iodine.** Sponge with clear cold water, then use alcohol or ammonia.

- **Mildew.** Wash item in cold water and borax.

- **Paint.** Sponge with turpentine. Wash item in mild soap in tepid water.

- **Rust.** Rust that has set in is very difficult to remove.

- Soak the rust stain in lemon juice, then dry the item in the sun to bleach out. Rinse thoroughly.

Or

- Rub a paste of vinegar and salt into the stain. Let stand 30 minutes, and then launder as usual.

Or

- Work a paste of cream of tartar and hot water into the stain. Let set; then launder as usual.

Or

- Boil five stalks of rhubarb (cut into ½-inch pieces) in one cup of water until soft. Strain the juice. Pour the hot liquid over the stain. Launder immediately. Rhubarb contains oxalic acid, an antidote for the brown stains found on many linens. Use caution when using any acid-based product. Weaken the solution before applying to the fabric.

- **Shoe Polish.** Try mild soap and water. If that does not work, try turpentine.
- **Tar.** The commercial product, Goo-Gone, works well for removal of tar on fabrics. After dabbing on product, wash item in warm soapy water.

Or

Dab benzene or naphtha soap onto the item.

Or

As a last resort, soak the item in gasoline or carbon tetrachloride. Wash in warm soapy water.

- **Vaseline.** Sponge item with kerosene or turpentine.

- **Wax.** Harden the wax by applying an ice cube to the spot. Gently scrape off as much as possible. To remove the remaining wax, place the fabric between two sheets of brown paper and press with a warm iron, moving the paper as it absorbs the wax.

    Colored wax can be difficult to remove. You may wish to consult a professional dry cleaner. Or you may try to treat such stains yourself by dipping a sponge into rubbing alcohol and dabbing it on the soiled area before washing the item.

- **Wine.** White-wine stains can usually be removed with a hot, soapy washing.

    - To treat red-wine stains, sprinkle salt on the area and immerse the item in cold water. If the spot remains, rub it out with salt before washing the item.
    - Another remedy for red wine is to saturate the area with club soda or a solution of baking soda and water.

OBTAINING A VINTAGE LOOK ON FABRICS

TEA-DYED METHOD

Bring three gallons of tap water to a boil in a 16-quart stainless steel pot. Fill your sink with cold water and soak the fabric. The fabric must be uniformly wet to accept the dye evenly.

Add eight ounces of loose black tea, tied in a muslin bag, to the boiling water. Boil for 30 minutes to an hour to achieve the darkest dye. Remove the tea sack from the water.

Wring out the fabric from the cold water. Add the damp fabric to the dye bath.

Turn off the heat and allow the fabric to steep for several hours or overnight. Agitate occasionally to ensure even dyeing and to check the color. When the fabric has reached the desired color (it will appear darker when wet), use tongs to remove it from the bath.

Rinse under cold water until the water runs clear. Gently hand wash with a mild detergent and rinse again.

COMMERCIAL PRODUCTS

The easier method is to use tan Rit dye, but this does not give the same aged look as the tea-dyed method.

FRAMING

- An image or object should be matted with equal space on top and sides and an extra 1/8 to ½ inch at the bottom for proper alignment.
- When using glass, place a mat board or spaces between the glass and the artwork to prevent humidity damage. Special glass is available to protect art against harmful ultraviolet rays.
- Matting, adhesives, and other framing materials should be acid-free. Non acid-free materials can cause deterioration of the artwork and unsightly brown rims at the edges of the mat and everywhere adhesives are used.

FRAMING NEEDLEWORK.

- Needlework should be framed with thought given to permanence. Avoid irreversible mountings, such as adhesives.

The English Royal Academy of Needlework studies revealed that the most damage occurs when needlework is framed under glass. Far from protecting it from dust and pollution, the glass actually speeds up fiber deterioration. They found that non-glare glass is more damaging than regular glass, which is more damaging than no glass at all.

- Sealing needlework between glass and a back dustcover deprives these fibers of necessary moisture. Glass interferes with the breathing and response of the fibers to the atmosphere, leading to dry, brittle fibers.
- Wool and linen, used in quality needlework, are natural fibers. Moisture is a natural element in the character of the fiber, and vital to its stability.
- Protective sprays are also harmful to fabrics. They coat the piece with plastic resin that repels moisture.

FURNITURE

PAINTED FURNITURE CLEANER NONTOXIC FORMULA

    1 teaspoon sodium carbonate

    1 gallon hot water

Test a small area of the furniture to ensure that paint will not be removed. Wash gently with solution, rinse with clear water.

REMOVING STAINS, WATER MARKS, WATER RINGS

- To remove the white rings left by wet cups or glasses, rub with a mild abrasive. First, try cigarette or cigar ashes moistened with a little cooking oil. Apply with your finger.

- If that does not work, try successively stronger steps:

  - Table salt and a drop of water

  Or

  - Silver polish or car polish

  Or

  - Make a paste of pulverized limestone powder and cooking oil and rub briskly with the grain of the wood using a soft cloth. Wipe frequently to compare and match the gloss of the repaired area with the original finish.

- Commercial products such as Antique Charm will work to remove white rings when used with fine steel wool (0000).

- White marks made by liquids on varnished surfaces can often be removed if rubbed at once with a cut lemon or a little vinegar. Rinse off with clear water. Polish dry.

- Darken white circles with the crushed meat of a pecan made into a paste.

- Erase superficial ink spots with oiled pumice on fine steel wool.

SCRATCHES

- To disguise a furniture scratch, crush pecan or Brazil nuts into a paste and rub into the wood.
- Dab some iodine over scratches in mahogany furniture.
- Choose a matching color of paste shoe polish. Rub polish into the scratch. Protect with furniture oil.

BURNS

- Burns are one of the most serious types of furniture damage. The following method of treatment requires care and patience, but should postpone the need to refinish the entire piece.

Clean the burn area by carefully scraping with a sharp knife or single-edged razor blade to remove all loose dirt and charred wood. The area should then be cleaned thoroughly with odorless mineral spirits on a cotton swab. Smooth the area with fine steel wool (0000) wrapped around a pencil or stick. Clean and sand with the wood grain using 320 or finer sandpaper.

After cleaning again, a matching stain should be applied to the area. When the stain has dried, stick-shellac that matches the wood finish should be applied to level the damaged area. Rub down the area with high-quality furniture oil.

HARD-TO-SAND AREAS TIPS

- To make a sanding strip, cut a strip of duct, electrical, or masking tape six inches longer than the sandpaper and center it on the back of the paper along one edge.

Fold the extra tape over the grit side as handles. Cut the sandpaper to the width of the tape.

- At carving and turnings, fold the sandpaper and fit the folded edge into the curve so that the grit smooths both faces at the same time. Use fine steel wool (0000) to get all the way into deep crevices.

- For hard-to-reach grooves or drawer tracks, use a deck of playing cards as a sanding block. Wrap the sandpaper around the deck, and then push the edge of the deck against the irregular object you want to sand. The playing card block will take on the shape of the object.

- Wrap sandpaper around a blackboard eraser when sanding a large area. Use the hard side for rough sanding and the soft side for fine sanding.

EBONIZER FORMULA

This formula will blacken any wood that contains tannin such as mahogany, walnut, cherry, or oak.

    1 fine steel wool pad (0000)

    2 cups cider vinegar

Put the steel wool pad in a small plastic or glass bowl. Add the vinegar and let sit for several days or until the steel wool dissolves. Caution: Do not cover the bowl. Gas from the reaction between the vinegar and the steel wool could possibly cause it to explode.

CONTINUED

To use the solution, sponge the solution evenly onto a sanded wood surface. If a second coat is desired, wet the wood liberally but evenly with tap water and let it sit for at least one hour before restaining. Allow wood to dry overnight before applying a finish.

FURNITURE CLEANER FORMULA

Removes surface dirt and grime from finished wood.

   1 cup boiled linseed oil

   ⅔ cup turpentine

   ⅓ cup white vinegar

Thoroughly mix all the ingredients in a large bowl. Apply to wood surfaces with a soft cloth, rubbing to remove dirt and excess polish. For badly caked-on dirt, use superfine (0000) steel wool. Store cleaner in a tightly covered jar out of the reach of children.

LOOSE CASTERS

- When casters on furniture drop out of their slot too often, remove them, pour melted wax into the holes and insert the casters before the wax cools. After the wax has set, the casters will not fall out again.

DARKENING BARE WOOD

- To darken bare wood, soak a plug of chewing tobacco in a pint of ammonia for one week. Strain the liquid through an old pair of pantyhose before mopping it onto the wood. *Note: I could not resist including this tip!*

CHANGING LIGHT BROWN OAK TO DRIFTWOOD GRAY

- To turn bare oak from light brown to driftwood gray, rub the wood with household ammonia. The tannic acid in the wood reacts with the solution to change the color permanently.

VENEER BUBBLES

- Moisture underneath veneer causes the glue to loosen and bubbles to occur. First, place a piece of cardboard or a towel folded several times over the bubble. Heat the spot using an iron set on medium heat. Place a heavy weight over the area until the glue has dried.

  Or

  Slice along the grain line of the wood through the bubble. Squeeze furniture makers glue under the slice and distribute around. Press firmly. Use a clean, damp cloth to remove any excess glue and pat dry. Place a heavy weight over the area until the glue has dried.

MUSTY SMELL REMOVERS

- Saturate cottonballs with pure vanilla. Place on a saucer in the furniture.

- Set out white vinegar in open dishes to destroy odor.
- Sprinkle fresh dry ground coffee inside furniture. Leave for a couple of days before vacuuming out the coffee grounds.
- Place a bowl or bag of baking soda mixed with your favorite essential oil in the bottom of a piece of furniture. Allow to remain in the piece for a week before removing.
- Cat litter will remove the smell from musty furniture. Sprinkle in drawers or bottom of furniture. Leave for several days, then vacuum.
- Use a new dryer sheet tucked in the drawers.

GLASSWARE

REPAIRING BROKEN GLASSWARE

- For very good pieces of glass, seek professional help.
- For minor repairs, melted alum is better than glue for mending glassware. It holds well and does not show.
- Super Glue works well for most clear glass since it has about the same refraction level as glass.
- Exercise extreme care when using any glass piece that you have repaired. It will never be a strong as the original. It is best to leave repaired pieces on a shelf to enjoy and not to use.

PICKING UP BROKEN PIECES OF GLASS

- Never use your bare hands to pick up broken glass. Little slivers are difficult to see and you could end up injuring yourself. Carefully sweep broken glass into a dustpan. Wrap the shards in newspaper and throw them out.
- To pick up tiny shards of glass, wipe all around the breakage area with a paper towel smeared with moist bar or liquid hand soap. Rinse with a water-soaked paper towel and wipe the area dry.

CLOUDY GLASS

- Antique decanters or bottles are sometimes stricken with a cloudy or frosty condition called glass sickness. This occurs when a liquid has been left in the container too long.
- Mix fine clay or sand with either water or denatured alcohol. Swish it around in the container until the blur disappears. If this fails and your glass is valuable, consult an expert in glass repair.
- If the piece is not very valuable you may also try these other solutions:

  - Fill the glass container with water. Add one or two tablespoons of ammonia, let stand overnight. Wash and rinse.

  Or

  - Shake tea leaves and vinegar around in the vessel. Wash and rinse.

  Or

- To clean stains in hard-to-reach places, such as the interior of a vase or decanter, pour in a little raw rice or unpopped popcorn. Fill the piece with water and shake gently.

Or

- Fill the piece you wish to clean with water and a denture-cleaning tablet.
- Swish a light coating of baby or lemon oil inside the vessel to disguise the cloudiness. This will not fix the problem, but it will disguise it for display purposes. Remember to wash the vessel with warm soapy water if you are going to use it for serving liquids.

CLEANING HARD-WATER STAINS

- Rub stains gently with scouring pad dipped in vinegar.

CRUSTY SEDIMENTS

- Crusty sediments that cannot be dislodged by ordinary soap and water may yield to a soaking for a couple of days in a mixture of vinegar and water, or washing soap and water. The sediment will usually yield to either the acid or the alkaline bath, depending on what caused the crusting.

HEAVY ENCRUSTATIONS ON BOTTLES

- This method involves the use of Muriatic acid, so caution should be used not only for your own safety, but also for the glass vessel you will be cleaning.

- Tools needed:

  - A bottle brush and a scrub brush with very stiff synthetic or metal bristles.
  - A pad of steel wool coarse enough to cut through the accumulation of material without marring the glass surface.
  - 18 percent commercial-grade Muriatic (Hydrochloric) acid. Extreme caution should be taken when handling acid. Protective glasses or goggles are recommended, and gloves of an acid-resistant material. The acid can be diluted with equal parts of water, but the weaker the solution, the longer it will take to soak the item.
  - A plastic, glass, or pottery receptacle large enough to hold the item completely covered with the acid without danger of spillage.
  - Tongs to transfer the item in and out of the acid bath.
  - Polishing compound, such as MAAS.

Wash the item inside and out to remove grime and dirt. Thoroughly soak the item in the acid solution, making sure that it is completely covered. Soaking time will depend on the amount of encrustation and the strength of the acid. Generally, it is better to soak the item overnight. A few hours in the acid bath usually will be sufficient to clean most items with a moderate amount of encrustation.

Remove the item from the acid bath with the tongs. Rinse with cold running water, both inside and out.

The action of the acid will have broken down the encrustations so that brushing with the scrub brush will clean most of the rest of the surface. Steel wool will clean around embossing, the outer portion of the mouth, and the difficult spots on the vessel.

The bottle brush will come in handy for the inside of the container.

Rinse again in cold water. Another short soak may be necessary.

Once you are satisfied with the cleaning of the surface, only the dullness needs to be removed. Rub the bottle with fine steel wool and MAAS.

After drying, polish with a soft cloth. Be sure to clean polish from around the embossing.

HOBNAILED OR DEEPLY ETCHED GLASS

• Use a well-lathered shaving brush to clean deeply etched or hobnailed glasses.

CARNIVAL GLASS

• A mixture of ½ cup ammonia and ⅛ cup white vinegar will safely clean carnival glass.

REMOVING GLASS STOPPERS

• Do not tap the stopper or the neck of the bottle or decanter. You will probably break one or the other. Run hot water over the neck of the bottle for a short time. This should loosen it enough to pull the stopper out. Never twist or push the stopper into the neck of the bottle. The friction created causes the stopper to tighten in the opening of the bottle. If this does not work, apply the following mixture:

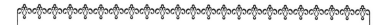

GLASS STOPPER REMOVAL FORMULA

½ teaspoon alcohol

¼ teaspoon glycerin

¼ teaspoon table salt

Cover the entire stopper and neck of the bottle with the mixture. Allow the mixture to soak for a few hours. Gently wiggle the stopper and remove it by lifting it away from the bottle. Rinse the stopper and the bottle in clear water. Dry both the bottle and the stopper thoroughly before inserting the stopper into the bottle again.

OTHER TIPS FOR GLASS

- Always use two hands to move pieces of glass, supporting the bottom. This especially applies to glass pitchers that are holding liquids.

- Do not store smaller glass objects inside larger ones, such as drinking glasses. Store smaller items in front of larger ones.

- Gilded decorations on glass are prone to wear. Wash these items by hand.

- Insert a spoon in a glass before pouring hot water into the glass. The spoon will absorb the heat and prevent the glass from cracking.
- Place a towel in the bottom of your sink when washing glassware. Also make sure that the faucet head is turned away from the sink basin.
- Try smoothing small nicks or rough edges in glasses with emery paper or an emery nail file.
- Do not expose glassware to extreme temperature changes. When moving glass from a warm area inside to outside cold and back into the warm area, allow the glass to adjust to room temperature before unpacking.
- Use Goo Gone to remove old labels, masking tape and sticky residue from glass.
- Dry glass with newspaper for a bright shine.
- Do not stack cut-glass pieces. This can cause small chiggers and chips that will devalue the pieces.
- Do not store liquids in crystal bowls or bottles for any length of time. This is one cause for "sick" glass.
- Never leave vintage glass in a sunny window. Glass made before 1900 can change colors. All glass can cause the sun to scorch draperies and furniture.
- Do not attempt to clean a paper label yourself. This is best left to a professional paper conservator.

GLUE: HOW TO CHOOSE

WOOD AND POROUS MATERIALS

Items made of wood, paper, leather, fabric, and other porous or absorbent materials are the ones most frequently in need of regluing. You have a choice of four main types of glue for use with these materials:

- White glue. This glue usually comes in plastic squeeze bottles of various sizes. It is inexpensive, sets in about one hour, and washes off with water while the glue is still wet. The most popular brands of white glue are Elmer's Glue-All and Franklin Evertite White Glue.

- Yellow Glue. This glue is stronger, fast-setting, and tackier than white glue. It can be sanded smooth when dry. The most readily available yellow glues are Elmer's Carpenter Wood Glue and Franklin Titebond.

- Waterproof glue for long-lasting outdoor use, as in repairing lawn furniture or exterior trim, requires mixing. Labeled either plastic resin or resorcinol resin, these glues are packaged with the necessary ingredients and instructions for mixing. The most common brands of waterproof glue are Weldwood Plastic Resin, Elmer's Waterproof Glue, and U.S. Plywood Waterproof Glue.

- Hot-melt glue comes in small stick cartridges that are inserted into an electrically heated applicator gun. Hot-melt glue sets as it cools, in less than a minute, and is waterproof. Most craft stores carry hot-glue guns and glue sticks.

- White and yellow glue come closest to all-purpose glue, but neither will adhere to nonporous materials, and neither is waterproof.

NONPOROUS MATERIALS

- Most plastic, metal, glass, rubber, and other nonporous materials can be glued together or to dissimilar materials if you use the correct glue. However, there are some plastics that seem to resist any type of adhesive.

- Silicone is a rubbery, flexible, waterproof adhesive that usually comes in a squeeze tube. It works on glass, china, wood, and metal, but will not adhere to vinyl or polyethylene.

IVORY OR BONE

- Ivory and bone are organic materials and become brittle with age and lose their natural color when exposed to intense sunlight. The golden color that ivory develops with age is natural patina.
- Dust or wipe old and brittle ivory with extreme care. Use an artist's soft bristle brush or a cosmetic brush. Washing old ivory or bone is not advisable.

JEWELRY

AMBER

- True amber, when rubbed with clean hands, will have a slight pine resin odor. However, you must have a good sense of smell to use this test.

- To determine if an article is true amber, mix four teaspoons of salt in an eight-ounce glass of water. Amber will float in this mixture. Imitation amber will sink.

  Or

- Rub amber on a wool carpet to build up static electricity. The amber will attract a small piece of paper or hair. Amber-colored glass will not.

- Amber will feel warm to the touch whereas glass will feel cold.

- Amber will also create a "clacking" sound when you tap it gently on your teeth, whereas glass will create a gritty sensation and a "clicking" sound.

CORAL

- True coral is made in large part of calcium carbonate. Do not expose coral to acidic liquids, such as vinegar, as it will effervesce and dissolve.

METAL COSTUME JEWELRY

- To prevent metal costume jewelry from tarnishing, store it with a piece of white chalk.
- Soak metal jewelry in diluted liquid detergent for five minutes to clean. Rinse in warm water and dry with a flannel cloth.
- Most fine jewelry cleaners contain either ammonia or alcohol. Do not use these cleaners on pearls or costume jewelry. Keep chemicals away from costume jewelry and treat it like fine pearls. Do not expose to alcohol, ammonia, hair spray, or perfume.

GOLD

- Gold will not tarnish if reasonably pure. Pure gold is 24K.
- Cleaning gold jewelry is a simple procedure. This works equally well for cleaning precious stones set in platinum.

- Fill a small bowl with any liquid soap and a teaspoon or more of clear ammonia. The ammonia adds luster to the gold and brilliance to any encrusted stones.
- Immerse the pieces in the bowl. Let stand for a few minutes.
- Remove one piece at a time. Using a soft toothbrush, gently brush the piece.
- Rinse the piece in a bowl of hot water. Be sure to close the drain if you rinse jewelry in a sink basin.
- Dry the piece carefully.

• Another method to clean gold without the liquid soap is to soak the jewelry in equal parts ammonia and lukewarm water for ten minutes. Rub with a soft brush and let dry without rinsing.

JADE

• Jade is cold to the touch. The term "Jade" is used generically for two materials: Nephrite and Jadeite. Nephrite comes from China and is softer than true Jadeite. Jadeite comes from Burma, Japan, Guatemala, California, Hawaii, Russia, and Switzerland.

• Jadeite comes in various colors—green, yellow, orange, and lavender—and has a greater translucent quality.

• To test for real jade, *carefully* rub the tip of a knife across the bottom of the item. If the mark is white, the item is not jade. If it leaves a black mark, it may be jade.

• Care is simple: wash jade with soap and water.

JET

- Jet is referred to as "black jewel" and is a type of coal that can be polished. Jet is a variation of one particular type of coal—lignite.

- Jet possesses a silky glow.

- Jet can be charged when rubbed. Rub jet on a wool carpet to build up static electricity. The jet will attract a small piece of paper or hair. Jet-colored glass will not.

- Victorian mourning jewelry made from jet became popular during Queen Victoria's time. Jet is a soft stone and should be cleaned by washing, drying, and rubbing it with fresh white bread.

PEARLS

- Pearls scratch easily and should be stored in an acid-free box or cloth bag.

- Pearls should be kept from contact with perfume and hairspray.

- Never wash pearls in anything but clear, cold water. Swish the strand gently; then dry with a soft towel.

- Do not allow perspiration or makeup to remain on pearls. Clean them immediately after contact with your skin.

- Have your pearls professionally restrung every few years, and be sure that they are knotted between each pearl.

PLASTIC JEWELRY

- Catalin and Bakelite plastic darken with age and with exposure to sunlight. Do not wear your plastic jewelry in the sun.

- Bakelite and Catalin jewelry should be wiped clean. If this does not remove the grime, use a soft abrasive cleaner such as MAAS. Buff gently, and then apply a small amount of beeswax furniture polish to retain the shine.
- Celluloid jewelry is very malleable and can be damaged by any exposure to moisture.
- Reference section on Plastics/Acrylics for cleaning methods for plastic jewelry.

GENERAL JEWELRY TIPS

- To determine if costume jewelry is plastic or glass, tap the piece on your teeth or touch it to your tongue. Glass will make a clinking sound or feel cold or gritty. This works for buttons too.
- Do not store jewelry in plastic wrap or plastic bags. Moisture buildup is harmful to all types of costume jewelry.

REMOVING GREEN MOLD ON JEWELRY

- Mix equal parts ketchup and mayonnaise. Dab onto the metal infected with the green mold. Leave on the piece for a few minutes and wash off. Reapply if necessary and leave on longer. Do not try this on jewelry with real or fake pearls.

LABEL REMOVAL

- Products such as rubber cement solvent, Bestine solvent, and Goo Gone will remove sticky labels, masking tape, and sticky residue left from labels on glass, pottery, and china.

- Be very cautious when using any product on paper. Test a small area before applying the product to a label to be sure that it will not leave a greasy spot. You can easily ruin a paper collectible by using these products. I have had great luck with Goo Gone, but I still test each time I use it on paper.

- For glass or china, peel away as much paper as you can. Next, soften the residue by applying vinegar, hairspray, nail polish remover, mayonnaise, or peanut butter.

- On painted surfaces, apply a hot rag or heat with a hairdryer. Be careful not to pull off the painted surface by working too quickly. You can reduce the value of a collectible item by removing the original paint.

- On plastic, apply a hot rag, rub gently with a dab of peanut butter, or heat with a hairdryer set on warm.

- On metal, rub gently with a dab of peanut butter. Carefully scrape off the softened residue with a dull table knife, a coin, a plastic letter opener, or your fingernail.

- On wood, cloth, pottery, or paper, use a hairdryer set on warm to soften the label.

SELF-ADHESIVE MOUNTS

To remove self-adhesive tape, drip vinegar behind the tape.

LACE

Historically important pieces of lace or linens with lace should be kept in their original condition. Museum curators prefer to conserve pieces as opposed to restoring them. Do not attempt to clean historically important lace. It shreds easily.

- Extreme temperature changes, moisture, direct sunlight, fluorescent lights, too little or too much humidity, plastic bags, and starch that can attract insects can easily damage delicate lace.
- To clean lace and linens that are in structurally sound condition:
  - Fill a sink basin with soft or distilled water.
  - Add two tablespoons of mild detergent and two tablespoons of a safe bleaching product. Not Clorox.
  - Use a colander or netting to swish lace around in the water. Lifting the water-weighted lace directly can cause thread damage.
  - Run water over the lace until it rinses clean.
  - When the lace is thoroughly rinsed, add ¾ cup of white vinegar to the basin of water to remove stains. Let soak a few minutes and rinse again.

   – To dry, roll the lace in a white towel to absorb moisture. Never wring or squeeze lace. Then lay the piece flat on a towel to dry.

- A slow-acting stain and spot remover, such as Lily-White Linens or Orvus, is safe for soaking lace that is structurally sound.

- Do not dry clean lace.

- Do not seal your linens or lace in plastic. The plastic prevents necessary air circulation around the fibers. If the piece is even slightly damp, mildew will start to form. Some plastics, when in contact with moisture too long, form hydrochloric acid that will eventually create holes in your fabrics.

- It is better to store linens and lace by laying them flat or rolling them on acid-free cardboard rolls or wooden poles covered in muslin.

- Fold linens and lace using a clean piece of cotton cloth between the folds.

- Periodically unfold and refold linens and lace along different lines to give the fibers stress relief.

LACQUERED ITEMS

- Clean lacquered trays, boxes, or furniture with liquid wax, applied with a clean cloth. Polish gently.
- Keep lacquered items away from heat sources.
- Lacquered items require a relative humidity level of at least 55 percent. Store small items in a cabinet near a small open dish of water.

LEATHER

- Vintage shoes, purses, and belts can all benefit from the following tips.
- Consult a professional for severe stains, but some remedies can be tried at home.
- Because leather readily absorbs moisture, wiping it clean with a wet rag only invites attack by mold and bacteria. Instead use a soft brush to wipe away dust and dirt.
- Loosen ground-in dirt with an artist's eraser that can be found at office or supply stores.

- Massage saddle soap into scuff marks with a clean, dry cloth. Work in circles until the scuff mark is gone. Gently buff with a soft cloth.

- The best way to preserve leather is by controlling its environment rather than altering the object itself. Avoid storing leather in excessively humid areas where mold and bacteria thrive. Likewise, leather stored in a dry area may crack or split.

- Keep leather away from heat sources, which deteriorate its protein content.

TREATING LEATHER

- Clean the leather first. Apply a small amount of castor oil with a soft cloth pad or with your fingertips. Rub the area well and remove the excess oil carefully with a clean cloth.

- If you get an oil or grease stain on leather, quickly blot up as much of the stain as possible. Then rub pure unscented talcum powder into the stain. Work it well into the leather. Remove the talc with leather cleaner such as Lexol-pH. If the remaining stain is still unsightly, darken the leather with mink oil to match the stain.

- Consult a professional for ink stains.

- Fill in scratches with indelible ink. Choose a few shades lighter than the leather, unless it is black, and apply conditioning cream immediately to help blend in the color.

LEATHER POLISH FORMULA

3 ounces beeswax

1 ounce white, bleached beeswax

1 pint pure turpentine

2 cups water

1 ounce pure soap flakes or shredded castile soap

   Bottles with tight stoppers

In a nonplastic container, shred waxes into turpentine. Cover and allow to dissolve. Or place turpentine and wax in a double boiler to warm until wax is dissolved. If using a double boiler, use extreme caution, as both wax and turpentine are flammable.

Bring two cups of water to a boil. Add soap and stir until dissolved. Let mixture cool. Add it to the wax/turpentine, stirring rapidly to prevent striation. Pour the mixture into bottles and seal. Always shake well before using. Use sparingly.

Rub vigorously with a shoe brush to renew color and shine on old leather wares.

LOUPE: HOW TO USE

- A loupe (pronounced *loop*) is a useful tool to examine everything from diamonds to cast iron toys. With a little practice, almost anyone can learn how to use it properly.

- For occasional use, it is more practical to hand hold a loupe away from your eye rather than learn to hold it to your eye like a monocle. Hand holding a loupe also means you do not have to remove eyeglasses, if you wear them.

- Hold a watchmaker's loupe between your thumb and forefinger.

- Hold a diamond loupe the same way, but also wrap your fingers around the lens housing to help support the loupe.

- If you are examining a small object, hold the object in your free hand. Brace your elbows against the sides of your body and bring both your hands up toward your face. You may brace your elbows on a table top if you are seated.

  As you raise your hands, bring the fleshy part of your palms (the heels) together. This creates a movable hinge. Keeping the loupe close to your eye, pivot the hand with the object in and out until you get a sharp focus. It is very important to brace yourself to insure a steady focus. If you cannot maintain focus, you cannot make accurate observations.

You will avoid eye strain by keeping both eyes open during an examination. This may seem awkward at first but comes easily with some practice.

MARBLE

Marble is porous and susceptible to stains. Although the surface appears hard, marble is easily scarred and stained.

- Moisture from glasses, flower vases, or alcohol leaves stains that are often difficult, if not impossible, to remove. Use coasters on furniture if placing any water-filled items on the piece.

- To polish marble, use chalk moistened with a little water and apply friction. Use only on polished, not honed or dull-finished marble.

- Marble is subject to rust stains. Several commercial agents are sold that remove rust stains from marble. Use these products as directed or you may damage your marble beyond repair.

- Do not use acids on stains. The marble will dissolve.

- Try covering stains on marble with Hydrogen Peroxide USP 3 percent. Allow to set for several hours. Repeat if necessary. This method has proven effective and is harmless.

NONABRASIVE MARBLE CLEANING FORMULA

¾ cup sodium sulfate

¼ cup sodium sulfite

Mix both ingredients in a small bowl. Sprinkle on marble and rub with a damp sponge. Wipe surface clean. Store the mixture in a tightly covered, labeled jar out of the reach of children.

METALS: IDENTIFYING WITH A MAGNET

WILL ATTRACT A MAGNET:

Ferrous metals such as:

    Cast Iron

    Iron

    Iron covered in brass

    Nickel (pure, not the coin)

    Steel (carbon or cast)

    Tin (some are and some aren't)

    Wrought iron

WILL NOT ATTRACT A MAGNET:

Nonferrous metals such as:

Aluminum	Lead
Solid brass	Pewter without lead content
Bronze	Pot metal
Copper	Stainless steel
Chrome	Sterling silver
Gold	

MILDEW CLEANER

High humidity and warmth contribute to the growth of mildew and mold. The best way to inhibit growth of mold or mildew is to reduce humidity. Increase air flow with fans, open windows, air conditioners, and dehumidifiers.

- A solution of one part household bleach and four parts water will kill surface mildew. If possible, put the affected piece outside in the shade on a breezy day.
- Scrub mildew spots with baking soda or borax.

  Or
- Sponge with white vinegar.

  Or
- Scrub with a paste of lemon juice or white vinegar and salt.

Mirrors

- Never resilver the glass on an antique mirror if you want to retain its monetary value as an antique. Enjoy its age and its value as an antique.
- After washing mirrors or picture glass with soap and water, crumple up newspaper and wipe the glass dry. It will sparkle and be streak free.

Nickel

- Clean nickel with soap and water. Rinse and polish with a soft cloth. If this does not work to your satisfaction, use whiting, or a fine cleaning powder moistened with alcohol. Rinse and polish. Nickel darkens if it is not cleaned frequently.

Paper Collectibles

Consult a paper restorer for rare paper articles. Dealers and collectors also refer to paper collectibles as *ephemera*.

- Maintain a constant temperature in the room where paper collectibles are stored. Temperatures of 60–70 degrees Fahrenheit and a relative humidity between 40 and 50 percent.
- Wear cotton gloves when handling paper items to protect paper from perspiration, oils, stains, and acidity.
- Remove creases and surface dirt from paper collectibles before framing and displaying the items.

- Use a bone folder to remove creases from paper documents. Begin in the center of the document and press the bone folder lightly along the back of the crease in a outward direction and toward the edge of the paper. Frame the document when it is flat and clean.

- To clean a document, put on cotton gloves and sprinkle Opaline on the soiled document. Opaline is a nonabrasive, light cleaning agent that can be obtained at art supply stores. Rub erasures lightly in a circular motion, and brush away soiled particles with a soft-bristle artist's brush.

- Do not glue or tape paper collectibles in an album or scrapbook. Adhesives leave permanent stains on paper. Use paper or photo mounting corners.

- Common items should be repaired with ordinary household white glue applied carefully with a toothpick. For easier application, thin the glue with water before applying. Blot any excess glue with a paper towel.

- If paper collectibles become infested with bugs, seal them in plastic bags and store them in the freezer for three days. This will kill the bugs and not harm the paper.

- Store paper collectibles away from direct light.

- Store paper collectibles in acid-free materials.

- Never trim a document to fit in a frame or mat board.

- Never display framed materials in direct sunlight.

- Never use tape, staples, or paper clips (metal or plastic) on valuable documents when stored in file folders.

- Never permit a framed document to remain in contact with the frame glass. Use an acid-free mat board to allow air to circulate between the glass and the paper. Use spacers between paper, mat, and frame.

- Never write on a document, even in pencil.
- Never attempt to erase any writing that is already on a document. View the writing as part of its history.

Pewter

- Old pewter likes a warm environment; if left constantly in an area where the temperature drops below 60 degrees Fahrenheit, pewter slowly disintegrates.

- Pewter is very soft. To clean, use a very mild abrasive so as not to create holes in the metal.

- Many collectors have confused dirt and grime with true patina. Removing dirt with soap and water will not remove the patina of old pewter. Pewter should be polished with nothing more coarse than super-fine steel wool (0000) and a metal polish specifically made for pewter. Be sure enough lubricant is on the steel wool so as to prevent scratching. Rub only in the direction of any skimming mark left by the pewterer's tool. Wash off polish residue using a mild soap and warm, flowing water. Dry, then buff by hand with soft, clean cloths and pewter polish until the cloth no longer turns black.

- Modern pewter can be maintained by washing with soap and water. Never use steel wool or harsh abrasives on modern pewter. The finish will be ruined.

PEWTER CLEANER NONTOXIC FORMULA

2 tablespoons pulverized limestone powder (also called rottenstone, available at hardware stores)

small amount of vegetable or olive oil

few drops of vinegar

Make a paste of the above ingredients. Rub until the metal looks bright. Wash and polish dry.

PEWTER CLEANER NONTOXIC FORMULA

2 teaspoons salt

2 teaspoons flour

2 teaspoons vinegar

Mix ingredients together to form a paste. Apply to the piece and let the mix dry. Wash with warm, sudsy water. Rinse thoroughly and buff dry.

LOW GLOW PEWTER CLEANER FORMULA

Use liquid soap and water. Dry with soft cotton or linen cloth.

BRIGHT FINISH PEWTER NONTOXIC POLISH FORMULA

Make a paste of whiting and denatured alcohol. Let the paste dry on the pewter, then polish. Wash, rinse, and dry.

MORE NONTOXIC FORMULAS

- Use wood ashes moistened with water.

  Or

- Rub with raw cabbage leaves and buff with a soft cloth.

  Or

- Remove corrosion from old pewter with super fine (0000) steel wool dipped in linseed, olive, or vegetable oil.

PHOTOGRAPHY

- Store photographs in a cool, dry place away from sunlight, the air conditioning, a hot lamp, or a heating unit.

- Before handling photographs, wash your hands, or wear light cotton gloves.

- Use pencil and a light touch or a marking pen made for photographs to write on the back of photographs. Do not use regular ink, felt-tip pens, or rubber stamps as they can bleed through to the image itself.

- Mount small snapshots with photograph corners. Use paper hinges with archival glue or tape (pH balanced) for larger photographs. Do not use regular cellophane tape, masking tape, synthetic glue, adhesive, or rubber cement.

- Select albums either with pages of archival plastic like Mylar (it doesn't have that plastic smell); acid-free paper with interleaving tissue to prohibit contact of photographs on facing pages; or sheet protector pages of acid-free paper covered with archival plastic. Magnetic photograph albums are especially harmful to color images, as the pages contain acid and adhesive that will bleed through the photograph's paper backing.

- Keep negatives and prints separate; they contain chemicals that are mutually harmful.

- Take folded, stained, or brittle prints to your nearest museum or paper conservator for special handling by a professional. If you try to unfold a print, it may tear.

- Color film and photographs deteriorate about four times faster than black-and-white.

PLASTICS

For this section we will use the generic word *plastic* to describe Celluloid, Lucite, Plexiglas, Bakelite, Catalin, and other polymer acrylic products.

Celluloid, the first synthetic plastic material, was developed in the 1860s and 1870s from a formulation of nitrocellulose and camphor. It is a moldable material that was capable of low-cost production in a variety of colors. Celluloid was made into toiletry articles, novelties, photographic film, and many other mass-produced goods. Celluloid is highly flammable and its popularity began to wane toward the middle of the 20th century, following the introduction of plastics based entirely on synthetic polymers. Lucite and Plexiglas are trademarked names of synthetic, colorless, and highly transparent materials with high stability and good resistance to weathering and to shock. Lucite and Plexiglas can be tinted or rendered opaque by the addition of other substances. They are usually fabricated by molding into solid articles or casting into sheets. Bakelite, invented in 1907, is a phenolic resin used for making vintage radio cases, jewelry, kitchen utensils, and a myriad of other highly collectible items. Catalin is a tradename for another phenolic resin that later competed with Bakelite.

CLEANING PLASTICS

- Do not use abrasives when cleaning plastics, especially Lucite or Plexiglas as they can scratch the surface.
- Wash with mild soap or detergent, with plenty of luke-warm water, and dry with soft cloth or chamois.
- Goo Gone works wonders on plastics.
- Grease, tar, or oil can be removed with hexane or kerosene. Solvent residue should be removed by washing immediately.
- DO NOT use window cleaning sprays, scouring compounds, acetone, gasoline, benzene, carbon tetrachloride, or lacquer thinner to clean plastics.
- Wax will help hide scratches that may appear. Buffing may help remove deep scratches. Anti-static polishes are available for acrylics.
- Brilliantize is the product recommended by Plexiglas dealers and experts for cleaning and shining Plexiglas. Do not use Windex or other glass cleaners on Plexiglas.
- MAAS Polishing Creme is a good polish also recommended for polishing and buffing out slight scratches on the surface of plastics.
- Avoid sunlight for Bakelite and Catalin.
- See sections in book on Buttons for more tips on the care of plastics.

CLEANING COUROC TRAYS/PLATES

Couroc is a brand name for a black phenolic resin product that was started in 1946 and was produced until the 1990s. They are highly collectible, serviceable, beautiful, and underrated. They often have natural materials such as coral and shells imbedded.

- Use MAAS to polish to a shiny finish. Wash with warm sudsy water. Dry thoroughly.
- Do not use pieces for cooking. They are for serving only and can be damaged by excessive heat.
- Can become brittle and color may deteriorate or change when exposed to ultraviolet light. Keep away from strong light and pollution.

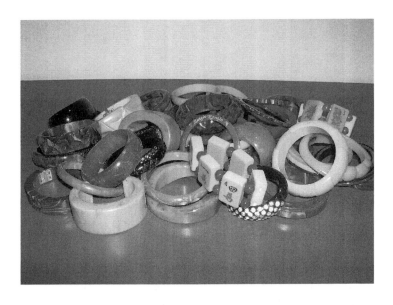

HOW TO DETERMINE IF A PLASTIC ITEM IS BAKELITE OR CATALIN

- Using a soft cloth, rub a small amount of MAAS Polishing Creme on an inconspicuous place on the piece to be tested. MAAS is a pale pink color. The cloth will turn a yellow-gold shade if the object is Bakelite or Catalin. It does not matter what color the object is, the cloth will turn yellow-gold.

If not, it is highly likely that the piece is not Bakelite or Catalin.

If the item is dyed you may remove some of the color, so be sure to test a small inconspicuous spot first.

If there is metal trim, you may notice that part of the cloth turns black. This may be caused from removal of tarnish from the metal. Test a spot that does not have metal trim.

POSTAGE STAMPS

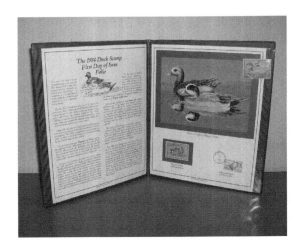

Philately is the study and collection of postage stamps. It derives from the Greek word meaning "love of what is free of further tax." Collecting stamps is one of the most popular categories of collecting. The first British postage stamps were released in 1840 featuring Queen Victoria. The first United States postage stamps, a five-cent Ben Franklin and a ten-cent George Washington, were issued in 1847.

- To properly care for postage stamps you need:
  - A stamp album with acid-free pages
  - Mounts specifically made for affixing stamps to the album pages. Do not use adhesives, tapes, or glue.
  - Philatelic tongs for handling stamps. Avoid handling stamps with your fingers as oil, dirt, and crimped corners can diminish a stamp's value.

POTTERY

Pottery describes earthenware or stoneware made from clay. It is usually not translucent like porcelain or chinaware.

- Learn to use a black light to detect some of the invisible repairs that may have been made to your pottery. Many areas of repair will fluoresce under the ultraviolet rays of the black light.
- Using your forefinger, gently thunk the edge of a piece of pottery. If you hear a "dead" sound, it is likely that the piece has a hairline crack or chip.
- Never put older pottery or dinnerware into your dishwasher, where the chemicals, hot water, and rattling around could cause damage.

- Periodic dusting and a bath in a rubber pan filled with warm, sudsy water, should be all the care your pottery needs.
- Be particularly careful with gilding. Water and washing may wear off these glazes.
- Support your ceramic pieces with both hands when lifting. Do not lift by a handle.
- Periodically check your shelves to be sure that your pottery has not "walked" too close to the edge.
- Use bubble wrap, paper plates, or cloth between plates if you must stack them.

QUILTS

CLEANING TIPS:

- First of all, determine whether the quilt is sturdy enough to withstand cleaning. Stitches should be secure, batting firmly enclosed by the quilt's top and backing, and fabric should not be torn or deteriorated.

- If you are unsure whether to clean or wash a quilt, consult a textile conservation expert. Indiscriminate cleaning of a quilt may destroy it. Use caution before you try to do it yourself.

  You may be able to clean cotton or linen in your home. Wool or silk quilts can be dry-cleaned if the cleaner will do it by hand.

- Test for colorfastness by placing a few drops of water on a small corner of the fabric. Press firmly with a white towel. If the color appears on the towel, do not clean the quilt yourself. If no color appears, try again on other spots to be sure that all parts are safe. Next, try with a few drops of water and a mild detergent.

- Avoid washing an old quilt in the washing machine unless the quilt is in very stable condition. The twisting and agitation can break the threads and tear the fabric.

- Fill a bathtub half full with lukewarm water. Place an old sheet under the quilt to ease lifting it out of the tub. Fold in quarters and let it soak for about 30 minutes. Drain the tub without removing the quilt, then refill.

    Add a half cup of mild detergent or textile soap, such as Orvus. Gently agitate. Let soak for about 30 minutes. Drain and refill tub with cool water several times until all soap is rinsed away.

- Get help to lift the quilt out of the water: it will be very heavy and the pressure can tear the fabric and break the stitches.

- Dry the quilt *flat,* if possible outdoors on a clean sheet away from direct sunlight.

- In between washings, spread the quilt on a freshly vacuumed carpet. Cover with a sheet of fiberglass or plastic screening material. Vacuum with the brush attachment using the lightest suction.

- Do not use a commercial bleach—it will weaken fragile fibers.

    However, for colorfast quilts with yellow-brown age or fold stains and dinginess, Lily-White Linens is safe.

- For brown spots and yellowed areas on old quilts, add a few drops of lemon juice and distilled water to a touch of Orvus to form a runny paste. Wet the stained area, dab on mixture, and let it set for 15 minutes. Rinse the item thoroughly in warm water. Do not use the mixture on colored linens, as the acid in the lemon can lighten or remove the color.

- For all white quilts, follow same instructions for tub washing, but after washing with detergent, soak a final time with Lily-White Linens.

STORAGE TIPS:

- Store quilts in a stable environment where extreme humidity and temperature changes can be controlled.

- Never store a quilt in a plastic bag. Moisture gets trapped inside and can cause stains and permanent damage.

- Protect quilt with white pillowcases and sheets, which allow quilts to breathe; or use acid-free tissue paper or acid-free paper boxes.

- Do not store quilts on bare wooden shelves or drawers or in wooden trunks. Acid in the wood will leave stains and damage fibers. Line shelves, trunks, or drawers with acid-free paper, available at hobby or fabric stores.

- Refold quilts every three to four months to prevent permanent creases.

HANGING TIPS:

- Evaluate the condition of the quilt to determine its ability to withstand the weight.

- One of the most common ways to hang a quilt is to sew a fabric sleeve to its back. Measure a strip of fabric (white muslin or cotton is preferred) approximately two inches shorter than the width of the quilt. Make the strip wide enough (about eight inches) so that, when folded in half and sewn, a finished wooden rod, dowel, or slat will slip inside. Hem each end of the sleeve.

  Hand sew the top and bottom edges of the sleeve to the quilt. You should be able to hide the rod and hardware behind the quilt.

- Another decorative method is to sew a cotton tube so that you can cut eight to ten hanging tabs from it. You may wish to choose a coordinating fabric. Cut the tube into eight-inch sections; iron each tab in half. Hand sew each tab to the top of the quilt equal distances apart. Slip a decorative wooden dowel through all of the tabs.

- After a quilt hangs for six months, store it for six months.

- Seal wooden rods with paint, shellac, or varnish to prevent wood acids from damaging the textiles. Then cover the rods with cotton batting and muslin strips wound tightly around the rod.

Rugs

Professional conservators should be consulted about major restoration of antique rugs. If your rugs are in good condition, general care can be taken at home.

- To vacuum the rug, cover with a fiberglass screen to protect the fibers. Then sweep with a soft vacuum brush.
- If the rug requires washing, test for colorfastness by wetting a small portion with a little cold water. Blot the area with a clean white cloth. If the color does not bleed unto the cloth, the fibers should be colorfast. Dip a sponge in cold water mixed with a mild detergent and squeeze it almost dry. Dab the sponge on the surface of the rug in a circular motion. Work a small area at a time. Rinse by sponging with cold water. Do not let the water soak through to the backing.
- Do not expose a rug to direct sunlight.
- Protect the backing with a pad on the floor.
- When storing a rug, roll it loosely, front side out, and place in a clean, dark, dry area. Do not store in a plastic bag.

HOOKED RUGS

To clean a hooked rug, first try to vacuum thoroughly using a low-suction setting or sweeping the rug with a soft vacuum brush attachment.

- If that does not do the job, check for colorfastness before cleaning. A soft brush or sponge, cold water, and mild soap may be used to give a more thorough cleaning. Clean with a circular motion. Remove soap suds using a damp sponge.
- Foam carpet cleaners will also work well when you follow the manufacturer's directions.
- If deeper cleaning is necessary, the rug may be immersed in cold water using mild soap and a soft brush to loosen dirt. Rinse thoroughly. Lay the rug flat on a towel to dry, allowing one day per side.
- Never put an old rug in the washer or dryer.
- Do not beat or shake vigorously to remove dirt.
- Take precautions when using old hooked rugs on your floor. Do not place them in high traffic areas.
- When hanging rugs, be sure the weight is distributed evenly. Never use nails or staples on the rug. Instead, sew the rug onto a slightly larger cotton backing. Then attach the cotton backing to a frame with staples or tacks making sure they do not come into contact with the rug.

Rust

REMOVE RUST FROM METAL

- Remove small patches of rust with a typewriter eraser. It removes spots and won't scratch the surface.

REMOVE RUST FROM WROUGHT IRON

- Remove rust by rubbing with steel wood and kerosene. If very badly rusted, soak the piece in kerosene, then gently rub it with steel wool.

LOOSENING A RUSTY SCREW

- If you don't have oil, loosen a rusted bolt or screw with a few drops of any carbonated soft drink. The acid in the soda will break up some of the rust.
- Soak a corroded screw or bolt in vinegar for several days or until the rust begins to dissolve.

SILVER

- Sterling or electroplated silver is bound to tarnish. Tarnish is a brown discoloration caused by moisture and pollutants in the air. Regular cleaning, polishing, and use will help to prevent tarnishing.
- Store items not regularly used in tarnish-proof cloth bags obtained from department stores or jewelers.
- Salt, eggs, olives, perfume, salad dressing, sulfur, vinegar, and some fruit acids will cause spots, stains, or

corrosion. Immediately wash, rinse, and dry items that have come into contact with any of these.

- Hand wash your sterling pieces. Dry thoroughly with cotton cloths. Some sterling-handled knives are filled with tar. The heat from the dishwasher may cause the tar to expand and split the handles.

- Never wash stainless and sterling together. This will cause a chemical reaction that will tarnish the sterling and corrode the stainless.

- Do not use dishwashing powders or liquid containing salt as this will corrode silver.

- Mother-of-pearl, ivory, and bone-handled servers should never be put in the dishwasher.

- Although some sources suggest that it is safe to put sterling pieces in the dishwasher, the above warnings should deter you from this practice.

SILVER POLISHES:

- Rub with toothpaste on a soft cloth, rinse, and polish dry.
  Or

- Rub with a paste of water and cornstarch, or cigarette ashes, or baking soda with a damp cloth. Allow to dry. Polish with cheesecloth.
  Or

- Let silver stand in sour milk or buttermilk overnight (you can substitute 1 cup whole milk mixed with 1 tablespoon white vinegar or lemon juice). Wash and dry with soft cloth.
  Or

- To clean tarnished silverware in a jiffy, place it in a pan containing 2 quarts of water, 2 teaspoons of baking soda, and 2 teaspoons of salt. Bring solution to a boil and let silverware remain in pan for 15 minutes. Remove and rinse under cool water. Dry with a soft cloth.

SILVER WITH WOODEN HANDLES:

- Seal the handles with beeswax before hand washing. Try not to immerse the handles in water at all. Have loose handles repaired by an expert.

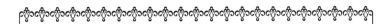

SILVER TARNISH REMOVAL FORMULA

This formula and method comes from the Museum of Fine Arts, Boston:

Precipitated calcium carbonate

Distilled water

Mild detergent such as Orvus, Ivory Liquid, or Joy

Soft cotton cloths

Cotton swabs with wood sticks

Cotton balls

Plastic wrap

Soft natural-bristle brush

Cover water-sensitive areas of silver objects with the plastic wrap. Make a slurry of about the consistency of thick cream of precipitated chalk in the distilled water. Apply in

CONTINUED

small quantities to silver with cotton and cotton swabs. Polish gently and in a circular motion. Discard cotton as soon as it is soiled.

Remove the chalk residue by washing surfaces with a very dilute solution of detergent in distilled water using the brush. Rinse with distilled water. Dry wet surfaces with soft, absorbent cloths. Dry trapped water in crevices with a hairdryer set on warm.

SILVER POLISH FORMULA

1 tablespoon salt

1 tablespoon baking soda

1 piece of aluminum foil

Place aluminum foil in a non-aluminum pan of warm water with salt and baking soda. Soak the silver object for about an hour. The smell of rotten eggs indicates that the tarnish is transferring itself onto the aluminum foil. Take the silver out of the solution and rinse in cool water. Rub stubborn spots with plain white toothpaste then wash in warm water and dry thoroughly. This method will remove all tarnish. If you like the antique look of dark areas in the crevices, do not use this method.

REMOVE SCRATCHES FROM SILVER

- Make a paste of putty powder and olive oil. Rub on with a soft cloth and polish with a chamois cloth.

TARNISH PROTECTION

- To prevent silverware from tarnishing, put an ordinary piece of white chalk in your silverware chest.

DON'TS FOR SILVER

- DON'T wrap silver in plastic bags or wrap, thinking this will keep silver from tarnishing. Plastic wrap will cause stains and otherwise damage your silver.
- DON'T use rubber bands around silver. Rubber will leave brown stains that even a silversmith will find next to impossible to remove.
- DON'T use the same polishing cloth on more than one metal. Residue from one type of metal can harm another.
- DON'T leave salt in salt shakers and cellars after use. Salt corrodes and pits silver quickly. Wash and dry shakers before storing.
- DON'T use commercial dips to clean silver with ornate detailing. They can remove the oxidation down in the ornate areas that is supposed to accentuate the fine details.
- DON'T use lemon-based detergent; it spots silver.

Steel

- Wash tempered steel immediately after use to prevent stains, and dry completely to prevent rust. Use scouring powder if necessary.
- Stainless steel is rust-proof, but if spots do appear, clean the utensil with fine steel wool or steel wool with scouring powder. Polish with a soft cloth.

Upholstery, Rug, and Carpet Cleaning

- Clean spills immediately with club soda.

  Or

- For red wine, tea, or coffee, cover the entire spot with a thick layer of salt. Let the salt soak up the stain, then vacuum up the salt.

  Or

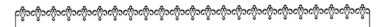

STAIN REMOVAL FORMULA

    1   quart of water

    1   teaspoon mild liquid soap

    1   teaspoon borax

        Squeeze of lemon juice or splash of vinegar.

Apply with a damp cloth or sponge and rub gently; wipe with a clean cloth and allow to dry.

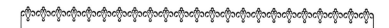

PET STAINS REMOVAL FORMULA

1 oz. clear ammonia

8 oz. cold water

Soak the area, allow to dry, repeat if stain persists. Do not use soap; it may set the stain.

Vintage Clothing and Textiles

See also the sections on Quilts, Fabrics and Textiles, and previous section for upholstery, for more specific information on these items.

STORAGE MATERIALS

- Store textiles and vintage clothing in washed, unbleached cotton or muslin.
- Use only acid-free tissue paper, and acid-free cardboard boxes. Use unbuffered tissue for all textiles and buffered only for cellulose fibers such as linen, cotton, jute.
- Old white sheets and pillowcases work well.

STORAGE METHODS

- If clothing is being stored for a long time, use a protective cover of cotton or a sheet.
- Place fabric in a wrapping of acid-free tissue before inserting in an acid-free box.
- Use acid-free boxes and store in a cool, dry place (under a bed is good). Do not use regular cardboard boxes.
- Place fabric in a wrapping of acid-free tissue before inserting in an acid-free box.

- Vary the way you fold textiles/clothing.
- Stuff the sleeves of coats, blouses, or dresses with acid-free tissue in order to prevent creases.
- Cover cardboard rolls with polyester or cotton batting and muslin wrapping.
- Check storage areas two to three times a year for insects.
- Use padded hangers that fit the shoulders of the clothing.
- Do not store vintage fabrics in plastic cleaners bags or plastic storage bags. Do not use zip-locked bags for small items. Moisture buildup can cause mold and mildew.
- Do not store fabrics that have been starched. They will attract silverfish and other pests.
- Sugar was a popular starching material in the old days. Remove sugar by washing the piece before storing (consult a professional for vintage fabrics). Critters love to munch on sugar-starched textiles.
- Do not store or display garments in sunlight. Bright light will fade the colors.

HOW TO PAD HANGERS

- Cut white cotton sheets or muslin into strips.
- Use wooden hangers, if available, because they are sturdier than plastic or wire.
- Avoid wire hangers altogether if you can.
- Cover the hanger with polyester or cotton batting material.
- Wrap the batting with cotton or muslin strips.

HANDLING VINTAGE TEXTILES OR CLOTHING

- If you are donning an antique dress, take off rings and other jewelry that may catch or snag fragile seams and fabric. Wear dress shields and extra undergarments such as a T-shirt and a slip. You may feel uncomfortable, but those extra garments can prevent damage from perspiration.
- Use gloves or wash your hands often.
- Use cotton thread to repair tears or holes.
- Never use safety or straight pins, paper clips, staples, or tape to repair garments. Those items can leave holes and rust marks.

WICKER

- The best way to clean old wicker is with a soft brush and warm soapy water. In between washes, dust pieces regularly with a soft cloth or the brush attachment on a vacuum cleaner.
- Vintage wicker left natural or coated with a clear lacquer finish is rarer and more valuable than painted wicker. Painted wicker can be stripped but make sure it is made of reed, rattan, or willow and not twisted paper or sea grass. It's best to consult a professional.
- To repair wicker, first clean it thoroughly. Remove flakes of old paint with a stiff brush and sand lightly with extra-fine paper. Paint with a quality enamel spray paint.
- To repair a loose frame binding, peel it a few turns and lightly spread glue on the frame. Rewrap and tape in place until dry.

Appendix A

AUCTION TIPS

- Try to attend the preview before bidding starts. Some auctioneers will point out flaws or imperfections, but don't depend on it. The preview is your opportunity to look for chips, cracks, and other problems before you bid.

- Check out box lots for hidden treasures. Before bidding, check to make sure the treasure you want is still in the box.

- Listen for the auctioneer's announcements before the bidding begins. You will learn the terms of the auction: method of payment; refund policy; if a buyer's premium will be added to the price; reserves applicable; "as is" terms; and return policies.

- Keep track of who is bidding so as not to bid against yourself. If the auctioneer notices, he should point this out to you; however, some unscrupulous auctioneers may take advantage of your mistake. Also, if you have a bidding partner, be sure you are not bidding against each other.

- At an estate sale, try to avoid bidding against relatives of the owner if it is evident that the item has sentimental value. Use your own judgment here.

- Keep your bid card ready so as not to delay the action. Hold your card high once you successfully win the bid so that your number can be recorded.

- Keep track of the items you win and the amounts you bid.

- When you leave the auction, take your number back to the check-out area, to avoid having your number used by someone else.

- Keep your wits about you. It is easy to be caught up in the excitement of the action.

Appendix B

Conducting a Successful Garage Sale

- Inventory your items. Be sure you have enough items and variety to be interesting. If not, invite some friends or neighbors to join in with you.

- Pick the right weekend. Give yourself enough time to prepare. If you plan a one-day sale, check whether Friday, Saturday, or Sunday is better in your town. (Oddly enough in our town, Friday is the better-selling day.) It is felt that two-day sales are more profitable, because they maximize customer availability.

- Advertise. Newspaper classifieds are important for success. Ask your local paper if they offer specials. It may be less expensive to run an ad more days than you need.

PREPARATION AND DISPLAY

- Clean items, hang clothes, fold items neatly, line up shoes, put clothes in one area, place books so that titles can be easily read.

- Borrow as many folding tables as you think you will need. Don't stack up items in boxes—they won't sell.

- If you have lots of similar small items that can sell for the same price, you may want to have 25¢, 50¢, 75¢, or $1.00 boxes.

- Have enough supplies. Gather bags and boxes, newspaper or plain newsprint paper to wrap items, masking tape, a measuring tape, pens and paper to keep track of sale items (especially if more than one of you is involved in the sale), a calculator, small change, and small denomination paper money.

PRICING

- Mark all your items. Nothing frustrates shoppers more than to have to ask how much something costs.

- Use stickers found at local discount stores. Don't use masking tape or other tape, as it is difficult to remove and may ruin paper or delicate items.

- Be sensible about pricing. Remember: unless you are selling only antiques and collectibles, you should not expect to make a profit. You are selling items you no longer need or want, and garage sale shoppers are expecting a bargain.

- Choose a mark-down time and let your customers know. Remove any items you don't want to mark down to rock bottom, and drop the prices on the rest. The idea is to get rid of the stuff, not to store it.

DON'TS

- Don't leave your cashbox unattended. A good "money box" is a fanny pack that you can wear on your body.

- Don't be the only one manning the sale. The first hour or so is always hectic for you and your customers.

- Don't leave any doors in your house open. Try to avoid letting anyone into your home unless you know them well.

- Don't place breakable items on high shelves. If a glass, pottery, or china item has a lid, tape it shut. Shoppers tend to turn things over to see who made them.

FINALLY

- Select a local charity to whom you wish to donate leftover items. Only keep the items you removed before your mark-down time. Inventory and box the rest and donate to a worthy cause. You will have a cleaned-out garage and a chance to write off your donation. A double bonus!

Appendix C

SMART SHOPPING AT GARAGE SALES

- Scan the local papers and plot your route the night before. Along the way watch for signs posted at intersections for those sales not advertised. Separate Friday, Saturday, and Sunday sales.

- Prioritize sales by merchandise that most interests you. Of course, keep in mind that if more than one sale is in a neighborhood, it makes sense to visit them together rather than backtrack.

- If you are interested in only one collectible, mention your interest to the people holding the sale. They may not have it out and would be willing to call you later. Don't dawdle.

- Wear a T-shirt depicting your collecting interest.

- Carry dollar bills and loose change. Carry bags, wrapping paper, batteries, and a measuring tape. Assume responsibility for wrapping your own items.

- Don't be afraid to bargain, but be polite: "Would you be willing to take less for this?" is a good way to ask. Ask if the price could be reduced if you buy several.

- Do not expect the homeowner to provide bathrooms and water. Use public facilities before you arrive.

- Be cheerful. You'll be surprised at how grateful the person holding the sale will be to encounter someone pleasant.

Appendix D

HAGGLING AT A FLEA MARKET

There are hundreds of flea markets in the United States today, each with its own personality. There are several unwritten rules of conduct that are followed at most flea markets.

- Try to be calm and examine items carefully for flaws, cracks, or repairs. This is easier said than done in the heat of the hunt.

- Courteously ask "Could you take any less for this?" Negotiating price is an expected part of the game when shopping at flea markets. This practice is spilling over to antique shops also, much to the chagrin of shop owners and dealers.

- To get better prices, shop late in the day (although most of the good items will have been picked over by then).

- Pay in cash rather than by check. You may be able to negotiate an even better price.

- Group items together and ask for a price for all of it. Do not focus too much interest on any one item.

- If you are very interested in an item, put your hand on it or pick it up. An unwritten rule is that the person touching an item has first claim.

- By the same token, respect the person who is negotiating for an item, even if you desperately want it. Do not make a higher offer while the other person is negotiating.

- Try not to shop alone, but don't shop with someone who has the same collecting interests as you. Let your shopping partner look over the item you are interested in to check for flaws, crack, or repairs that you may not have noticed in the excitement of the find.

- Determine your price range before negotiating with a dealer.
- Try to resist buying something you really want but cannot afford.
- Receipts at flea markets are not the norm. If you are buying an inexpensive collectible, most often the rule is BUYER BEWARE.

However, if you are buying an expensive item, ask for a receipt detailing what the object is, where it came from, when it was made, how it was made, and what materials were used to make it. Also write the dealer's name, address, and telephone number on the receipt. Any flaws, restoration, alterations, or repairs should be noted. (Repaired means using original parts; restored means using new parts.) "Money back guarantee, no questions asked" may allow you some recourse if you have a problem with your purchase.

This is important for insurance and possibly later for capital gains taxes. It is also important in case the item has been misrepresented (meaning it is not what the dealer represented it to be, or has been repaired with new pieces).

- Allow dealers to educate you (if they are willing to take the time). However, there is no substitute for educating yourself before you go shopping. Experience is the best teacher, but reading books, going to museums, attending antiques courses, and talking with reputable dealers and collectors will better prepare you for this unique shopping experience.

Appendix E

DATES TO REMEMBER

BRITISH REGISTRATION MARKS

"Rd" in a diamond-shaped registry mark indicates registration of a design at the Patent Office against copying between 1842 and 1883. The exact date the item was registered can be worked out from the letters and figures in the points of the diamond, but the articles so marked may have been manufactured considerably later. The information within the diamond changed after 1867.

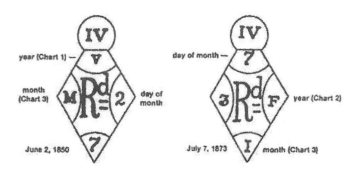

THE ROMAN NUMERAL AT THE TOP INDICATES THE CLASS OF GOODS, ACCORDING TO THIS CHART				
I	Metals	VIII	Other Shawls
II	Wood	VIII	Yarn
III	Glass	X	Printed Fabrics
IV	Ceramics	XI	Furniture
V	Paper Hangings	XII i	Other Fabrics
VI	Carpets	XII ii	Damask
VII	Printed Shawls	XIII	Laces

CHART 1		CHART 2		CHART 3 MONTH OF THE YEAR OF MANUFACTURE	
Letter	Year	Letter	Year	Letter	Year
X	1842	X	1868	C	January
H	1843	H	1869	G	February
C	1844	C	1870	W	March
A	1845	A	1871	H	April
I	1846	I	1872	E	May
F	1847	F	1873	M	June
U	1848	U	1874	I	July
S	1849	S	1875	R	August
V	1850	V	1876	D	September
P	1851	P	1877	B	October
D	1852	D	1878	K	November
Y	1853	Y	1879	A	December
J	1854	J	1880		
E	1855	E	1881		
L	1856	L	1882		
K	1857	K	1883		
B	1858				
M	1859				
Z	1860				
R	1861				
O	1862				
G	1863				
N	1864				
W	1865				
Q	1866				
T	1867				

BRITISH REGISTRATION FROM 1884					
Year	Number	Year	Number	Year	Number
1884	1	1913	612431	1942	839230
1885	19754	1914	630190	1943	839980
1886	40480	1915	644935	1944	841040
1887	64520	1916	653521	1945	842670
1888	90483	1917	658988	1946	845550
1889	116648	1918	662872	1947	849730
1890	141273	1919	666128	1948	853260
1891	163767	1920	673750	1949	856999
1892	185713	1921	680147	1950	860854
1893	205240	1922	687144	1951	863970
1894	224720	1923	694999	1952	866280
1895	246975	1924	702671	1953	869300
1896	268392	1925	710165	1954	872531
1897	291241	1926	718057	1955	876067
1898	311658	1927	726330	1956	879282
1899	331707	1928	734370	1957	882949
1900	351202	1929	742725	1958	887079
1901	368154	1930	751160	1959	891665
1902	385180	1931	760583	1960	895000
1903	403200	1932	769670	1961	899914
1904	424400	1933	779292	1962	904638
1905	447800	1934	789019	1963	909364
1906	471860	1935	799097	1964	914536
1907	493900	1936	808794	1965	919607
1908	518640	1937	817293	1966	924510
1909	535170	1938	825231	1967	929335
1910	552000	1939	832610	1968	934515
1911	575817	1940	837520	1969	939875
1912	594195	1941	838590	1970	944932

Continued

BRITISH REGISTRATION FROM 1884 *CONTINUED*					
Year	Number	Year	Number	Year	Number
1971	950046	1981	998302	1991	2012047
1972	955342	1982	1004456	1992	2019933
1973	960708	1983	1010583	1993	2028115
1974	965185	1984	1017131	1994	2036116
1975	969249	1985	1024174	1995	2044227
1976	973838	1986	1031358	1996	2053121
1977	978426	1987	1039055	1997	2062149
1978	982815	1988	1047499	1998	2071420
1979	987910	1989	1056078	1999	2080158
1980	993012	1990	2003720		

CENTURIES

The inventor of the current calendar, Pope Gregory, did not start with the year zero, so the first century went from 1 to 100. It is easy to tell the number of the current century: simply divide the final year of the century by 100. For instance: 2000 divided by 100 = 20, which is the 20th century.

Century	Years
1st	1–100
2nd	101–200
3rd	201–300
4th	301–400
5th	401–500
6th	501–600
7th	601–700
8th	701–800
9th	801–900

Continued

Century *Continued*	Years *Continued*
10th	901–1000
11th	1001–1100
12th	1101–1200
13th	1201–1300
14th	1301–1400
15th	1401–1500
16th	1501–1600
17th	1601–1700
18th	1701–1800
19th	1801–1900
20th	1901–2000
21st	2001–2100

CHINESE DYNASTIES AND EMPERORS	
Emperors, Ming Dynasty: 1368–1644 AD	
Hung-wu	1368–1398 AD
Chien-wen	1399–1402 AD
Yung-lo	1403–1424 AD
Hung-hs	1425–1426 AD
Hsuan-te	1426–1435 AD
Ch'eng-tung	1436–1449 AD
Ching-tai	1450–1456 AD
Tien-shun	1457–1464 AD
Ch'eng-hua	1465–1487 AD
Hung-chih	1488–1505 AD
Cheng-te	1506–1521 AD
Chia-ching	1522–1566 AD

Continued

CHINESE DYNASTIES AND EMPERORS *CONTINUED*	
Emperors, Ming Dynasty: 1368–1644 AD *Continued*	
Lung-ch'ing	1567–1572 AD
Wan-li	1573–1619 AD
Tai-chang	1620–1621 AD
T'ien-ch'i	1621–1627 AD
Ch'ung-chen	1628–1643 AD
Ch'ing (Qing) Dynasty: 1644–1911 AD	
Shun-chih	1644–1661 AD
K'ang-hsi	1662–1722 AD
Chung-cheng	1723–1735 AD
Ch'ien-lung	1736–1795 AD
Chia-ch'ing	1796–1820 AD
Tao-kuang	1821–1850 AD
Hsien-feng	1851–1861 AD
T'ung-chih	1862–1873 AD
Kuang-hsu	1874–1908 AD
Hsuan-t'ung	1909–1911 AD
Republic of China	
Republic of China	1911–1949 AD
People's Republic of China Chairman Mao Zedong	October 1, 1949–Present 1949–1976

JAPANESE PERIODS	
Jomon Period	ca. 10,000–300 BCE
Yayoi Period	ca. 300 BCE–300 AD
Kofun Period	ca. 300 AD–552 AD
Asuka Period	ca. 552–645
Nara Period	ca. 645–794

Continued

JAPANESE PERIODS *CONTINUED*	
Heian Period	ca. 794–1185
Kamakura Period	ca. 1185–1337
Muromachi Period	ca. 1338–1573
Momoyama Period	ca. 1573–1615
Edo Period	ca. 1615–1868
Meiji Period	1868–1912
Taisho	1912–1926
Showa	1926–1989
Heisei	1989–Present

"MADE IN JAPAN"	
1891–1921	Nippon
1921–1941	Japan
1941–1945	War Years, items not imported to U.S.
1945–April 28, 1952	Japan, Made in Japan, Occupied Japan, Made in Occupied Japan
1952–present	Japan

POSTAL ZONE NUMBERS AND ZIP CODES

Postal zone numbers were introduced between 1943 and 1963 as a one- or two-digit number following the city name. Postal zones were instituted in 1943 during WWII because many postal clerks had gone into the service and the inexperienced replacement postal clerks had difficulty sorting the mail.

By 1963, the Post Office Department devised a plan to speed handling and delivery of letter mail. The ZIP (Zone Improvement Plan) Code went into effect on July 1, 1963, allowing automated mailing systems to sort by the five-digit zip codes. This permitted private and business mailings to bypass as many as six mail-handling steps. The +4 zip code was introduced in October 1983 in hopes that the additional digits would further efficiency within the system. It didn't.

POSTAL ZONE NUMBERS AND ZIP CODES	
Prior to May 1943	no numbers
May 1943–July 1963	1 and 2-digit postal zone numbers following the city name
July 1963–September 1983	5-digit zip codes
October 1983–present	+4 zip codes (5-digit plus 4 additional)

POSTAL RATE CHANGES

Knowing the postal rates can help date letters and postcards where the cancellation mark with date is not legible. Postcards were first used in the United States in 1873.

POSTAL RATE CHANGES		
Effective Date	First Class Letter in Cents	Postcard in Cents
March 3, 1863	3 per half oz.+3 per half oz.	na
1873	3 per half oz.+3 per half oz.	1 cent pre-stamped United States Postal Card introduced
October 1, 1883	2 per half oz.+2 per half oz.	1
July 1, 1885	2 per oz.+2 for each additional oz.	2
1898–1916	2 per ounce+2 for each additional oz.	1
November 3, 1917–July 1, 1919	3+3 for each additional oz.	1
July 1, 1920–July 5, 1932	2+2 for each additional oz.	1

Continued

POSTAL RATE CHANGES *CONTINUED*		
Effective Date	**First Class Letter in Cents**	**Postcard in Cents**
July 6, 1932	3+3 for each additional oz.	1
January 1, 1952	3+3 for each additional oz.	2
August 1, 1958	4+4 for each additional oz.	3
January 7, 1963	5+5 for each additional oz.	4
January 7, 1968	6+6 for each additional oz.	5
May 16, 1971	8+8 for each additional oz.	6
May 2, 1974	10+10 for each additional oz.	8
September 14, 1975	10+9 for each additional oz.	7
December 31, 1975	13+11 for each additional oz.	9
May 29, 1978	15+13 for each additional oz.	10 (A Stamp)
March 22, 1981	18+17 for each additional oz.	12 (B Stamp)
November 1, 1981	20+17 for each additional oz.	13 (C Stamp)
February 17, 1985	22+17 for each additional oz.	14 (D Stamp)
April 3, 1988	25+20 for each additional oz.	15 (E Stamp)
February 3, 1991	29+23 for each additional oz.	19 (F Stamp)
January 1, 1995	32+23 for each additional oz.	20 (G Stamp)
January 10, 1999	33+22 for each additional oz.	20 (H Stamp)
January 7, 2001	34+21 for each additional oz.	20 Nondenominated
July 1, 2001	34+23 for each additional oz.	21 Nondenominated
June 30, 2002	37+23 for each additional oz.	23
January 8, 2006	39+24 for each additional oz.	24
May 14, 2007	41+17 for each additional oz.	26
April 12, 2007	First "Forever" stamp issued for 41 cents*	
May 12, 2008	42+17 for each additional oz.	27
May 11, 2009	44+17 for each additional oz.	28
April 17, 2011	44+20 for each additional oz.	29
January 22, 2012	45+20 for each additional oz.	32

*Forever stamps are always sold at the current first-class postage rate. They are always valid for the full first-class postage regardless of any rate increases since the stamps' purchase. Unused "forever" stamps purchased in April 2007 therefore are valid for the current full 44 cent first-class postage rate, despite having been purchased for 41 cents.

TELEPHONE NUMBERS

Although many men experimented with telephonic devices from 1844 on, it was Alexander Graham Bell who is credited with inventing the first practical telephone. In 1876, Bell was also the first to obtain a patent for his "apparatus for transmitting voice." His assistant, Thomas Watson, also became famous because of the well-known story of Bell's first words, "Mr. Watson, come here. I want to see you."

For many years telephone conversations were connected through a switchboard where the caller could simply ask to be connected to the person they were calling by name. However, this became impractical as telephones became more popular.

TELEPHONE NUMBERS	
1920s–mid 1960s	Use of exchanges of two letters followed by numbers, eg WHitney 7-5789 for the numbers 947-5789. It was believed that pronounceable words proceeding numbers would make it easier to memorize telephone numbers.
1930s–1940s	2–4 digit numbers
1940s–1960s	4–7 digit numbers. Exchanges dropped.
November 10, 1951	3-digit area code added to 7

Note: Did you ever wonder why on television and movies and in literature the telephone numbers often start with 555 (KLondike) 5? Starting in the 1920s, the 555 numbers have been reserved for that purpose and are not assigned to individuals so as not to have telephone customers bothered by thousands of random telephone calls from viewers.

CELLULAR TELEPHONES

The technology for the first crude mobile (car) phone was introduced in 1947. However, the FCC did not encourage the development of the technology. Dr. Martin Cooper, formerly with Motorola, is credited with inventing the first modern portable handset. Dr. Cooper made the first call to a rival at Bell Laboratories. The FCC, however, did not authorize the first commercial cellular phone service until 1982. By 1987, one million users of cell phones existed. Nearly 5 billion users had cell phones by 2011.

THE INTERNET

1950s–1960s	Point-to-point communications between computers started
late 1960s–1970s	Packet switched networks led to internetworking
1989	America Online (AOL) introduced
1991	worldwide web (www)
1995	Amazon, Craigslist, and eBay introduced
1996	Hotmail introduced
1998	Google Search introduced
1999	Napster introduced
2001	Wikipedia introduced
2003	Skype, Myspace, and iTunes introduced
2004	Facebook, Podcast, Flickr introduced
2005	YouTube introduced
2006	Twitter introduced
2009	Bing introduced

UNITED STATES INVENTION PATENTS

Invention patents usually cover how and why things work. This chart should help determine the date represented by US government patent numbers that started in 1836. The single number after each date indicates the beginning number for that year. For the year 1862, for example, the numbering begins at 34,045 and includes all numbers until it reaches 37,265; 37,266 starts the year 1863. This pattern continues through year 2009.

The granting of a patent gives the inventor exclusive rights to the manufacture, use, and sales of his invention for a period of 17 years. Terms commonly used for invention patents include "Patented," "patent," "ptnd.," "PAT'D," and "Pat No."

UNITED STATES INVENTION PATENTS					
Year	Number	Year	Number	Year	Number
1836	1	1852	8,662	1868	72,959
1837	110	1853	9,512	1869	85,503
1838	546	1854	10,358	1870	98,460
1839	1,061	1855	12,117	1871	110,617
1840	1,465	1856	14,009	1872	122,304
1841	1,923	1857	16,324	1873	134,504
1842	2,413	1858	19,010	1874	146,120
1843	2,901	1859	22,477	1875	158,350
1844	3,395	1860	26,642	1876	171,641
1845	3,873	1861	31,005	1877	185,813
1846	4,348	1862	34,045	1878	198,733
1847	4,914	1863	37,266	1879	211,078
1848	5,409	1864	41,047	1880	223,211
1849	5,993	1865	45,685	1881	236,137
1850	6,981	1866	51,784	1882	251,685
1851	7,865	1867	60,658	1883	269,820

Continued

UNITED STATES INVENTION PATENTS *CONTINUED*					
Year	Number	Year	Number	Year	Number
1884	291,016	1913	1,049,326	1942	2,268,540
1885	310,163	1914	1,083,267	1943	2,307,007
1886	333,494	1915	1,123,212	1944	2,338,081
1887	355,291	1916	1,166,419	1945	2,366,154
1888	375,720	1917	1,210,389	1946	2,391,856
1889	395,305	1918	1,251,458	1947	2,413,675
1890	418,665	1919	1,290,027	1948	2,433,824
1891	443,987	1920	1,326,899	1949	2,457,797
1892	466,315	1921	1,364,063	1950	2,492,944
1893	488,976	1922	1,401,948	1951	2,536,016
1894	511,744	1923	1,440,362	1952	2,580,379
1895	531,619	1924	1,478,996	1953	2,624,046
1896	552,502	1925	1,521,590	1954	2,664,562
1897	574,369	1926	1,568,040	1955	2,698,434
1898	596,467	1927	1,612,700	1956	2,728,913
1899	616,871	1928	1,654,521	1957	2,775,762
1900	640,167	1929	1,696,897	1958	2,818,567
1901	664,827	1930	1,742,181	1959	2,866,973
1902	690,385	1931	1,787,424	1960	2,919,443
1903	717,521	1932	1,839,190	1961	2,966,681
1904	748,567	1933	1,892,663	1962	3,015,103
1905	778,834	1934	1,941,449	1963	3,070,801
1906	808,618	1935	1,985,878	1964	3,116,487
1907	839,799	1936	2,026,516	1965	3,163,865
1908	875,679	1937	2,066,309	1966	3,226,729
1909	908,436	1938	2,104,004	1967	3,295,143
1910	945,010	1939	2,142,080	1968	3,360,800
1911	980,178	1940	2,185,170	1969	3,419,907
1912	1,013,095	1941	2,227,418	1970	3,487,470

Continued

UNITED STATES INVENTION PATENTS *CONTINUED*					
Year	Number	Year	Number	Year	Number
1971	3,551,909	1984	4,423,523	1997	5,590,420
1972	3,631,539	1985	4,490,855	1998	5,704,062
1973	3,707,729	1986	4,562,596	1999	5,855,021
1974	3,781,914	1987	4,633,526	2000	6,009,555
1975	3,858,241	1988	4,716,594	2001	6,167,569
1976	3,930,271	1989	4,794,652	2002	6,334,220
1977	4,000,520	1990	4,890,335	2003	6,502,244
1978	4,065,812	1991	4,980,927	2004	6,671,884
1979	4,131,952	1992	5,077,836	2005	6,836,899
1980	4,180,867	1993	5,175,886	2006	6,981,282
1981	4,242,757	1994	5,274,846	2007	7,155,746
1982	4,308,622	1995	5,377,359	2008	7,313,829
1983	4,366,579	1996	5,479,658	2009	7,472,428

UNITED STATES DESIGN PATENTS

Design patents usually cover how things are to be made. This chart should help determine the date represented by U.S. government patent numbers that started in 1843. The single number after each date indicates the beginning number for that year. For the year 1862, for example, the numbering begins at 1508 and includes all numbers until it reaches 1702; 1703 starts the year 1863. This pattern continues through 2009.

Patents for designs shall be granted for 14 years from the date of grant. Terms commonly used for design patents include: Design #, Patent Design, DSN #, Pat D, and Pat Ds.

UNITED STATES DESIGN PATENTS					
Year	Number	Year	Number	Year	Number
1843	1	1845	27	1847	103
1844	15	1846	44	1848	163

Continued

\multicolumn{6}{c}{UNITED STATES DESIGN PATENTS *CONTINUED*}					
Year	Number	Year	Number	Year	Number
1849	209	1879	10975	1908	38980
1851	341	1880	11567	1909	39737
1852	431	1881	12082	1910	40424
1853	540	1882	12647	1911	41063
1854	626	1883	13508	1912	42073
1855	683	1884	14528	1913	43415
1856	753	1885	15678	1914	45098
1857	860	1886	16451	1915	46813
1858	973	1887	17046	1916	48358
1859	1075	1888	17995	1917	50117
1860	1183	1889	18830	1918	51629
1861	1366	1890	19553	1919	52836
1862	1508	1891	20439	1920	54359
1863	1703	1892	21275	1921	56844
1864	1879	1893	22092	1922	60121
1865	2018	1894	22994	1923	61748
1866	2239	1895	23922	1924	63675
1867	2533	1896	25037	1925	66346
1868	2858	1897	26482	1926	69170
1869	3304	1898	28113	1927	71772
1870	3810	1899	29916	1928	74159
1871	4547	1900	32055	1929	77347
1872	5452	1901	33813	1930	80254
1873	6336	1902	35547	1931	82966
1874	7083	1903	36187	1932	85903
1875	7969	1904	36723	1933	88847
1876	8884	1905	37280	1934	91258
1877	9686	1906	37766	1935	94179
1878	10385	1907	38391	1936	98045

Continued

	UNITED STATES DESIGN PATENTS *CONTINUED*				
Year	Number	Year	Number	Year	Number
1937	102601	1962	192004	1987	287540
1938	107738	1963	194304	1988	293500
1939	112765	1964	197269	1989	299180
1940	118358	1965	199955	1990	305275
1941	124503	1966	203379	1991	313301
1942	130989	1967	206567	1992	322878
1943	134717	1968	209732	1993	332170
1944	136946	1969	213084	1994	342818
1945	139862	1970	216419	1995	353932
1946	143386	1971	219637	1996	365671
1947	146165	1972	222793	1997	377107
1948	148267	1973	225695	1998	388585
1949	152235	1974	229729	1999	403485
1950	156686	1975	234033	2000	418273
1951	161404	1976	238315	2001	435713
1952	165568	1977	242881	2002	452599
1953	168527	1978	246811	2003	468073
1954	171241	1979	250676	2004	484671
1955	173777	1980	253796	2005	500396
1956	176490	1981	257746	2006	513356
1957	179467	1982	262495	2007	534331
1958	181829	1983	267440	2008	558426
1959	184204	1984	272009	2009	584026
1960	186973	1985	276949		
1961	189516	1986	282020		

Appendix F

ROMAN NUMERAL INTERPRETER

Roman numerals are symbols that stand for numbers. They are written in certain capital letters of the English, or Latin, alphabet. The Roman numeral system was the most popular form of writing numbers until the widespread use of Arabic numerals in the late 1500s. All Roman numerals are written by combining seven basic symbols:

I = 1   C = 100
V= 5   D = 500
X = 10   M = 1,000
L = 50

There is no zero.

Roman numerals are written from left to right and almost all use the principle of addition. A person first writes the thousands, then the hundreds, then the tens, and finally the units. All 4's and 9's use the principle of subtraction, however. In Roman numerals, a smaller numeral appearing before a larger indicates that the smaller numeral is subtracted from the larger one. Thus 4 is written IV, or 5 minus 1; 9 is written IX, or 10 minus 1. Sometimes the rule of subtraction is not used, such as in the case of 400, which is written CCCC. To write larger numbers, a *viculum*, or bar, is sometimes placed over a number to multiply it by 1,000. For example, 15,634 is written $\overline{\text{XV}}$DCXXXIV.

ROMAN NUMERALS			
Modern Numeral	Roman Numeral	Modern Numeral	Roman Numeral
1	I	120	CXX
2	II	130	CXX
3	III	140	CXL
4	IV	150	CL
5	V	160	CLX
6	VI	170	CLXX
7	VII	180	CLXXX
8	VIII	190	CXC
9	IX	200	CC
10	X	300	CCC
11	XI	400	CCCC
12	XII	500	D
13	XIII	600	DC
14	XIV	700	DCC
15	XV	800	DCCC
16	XVI	900	CM
17	XVII	1,000	M
18	XVIII	2,000	MM
19	XIX	3,000	MMM
20	XX	4,000	$M\bar{V}$
30	XXX	5,000	$\bar{V}$
40	XL	10,000	$\bar{X}$
50	L	15,000	$\overline{XV}$
60	LX	25,000	$\overline{XXV}$
70	LXX	50,000	$\bar{L}$
80	LXXX	100,000	$\bar{C}$
90	XC	1,000,000	$\bar{M}$
100	C	5,000,000	MMMMM
110	CX	10,000,000	MMMMMMMMMM

Appendix G

INSURANCE AND ESTATE PROTECTION

BASIC RULE FOR YOUR ESTATE:

- Do not assume that your children, grandchildren, siblings, parents, or spouse know the value of your treasures. Take time to educate them or keep meticulous records.

GENERAL TIPS FOR INSURANCE:

- Read your insurance policy carefully. Each insurance company has variations from the standard form and coverage may vary.

GENERAL TIPS FOR INSURANCE AND ESTATE:

- Create an "estate" possessions register with photographs and values and put in a safety deposit box or wherever you keep your important documents.
- Use a digital camera or tape recorder—be sure to get a booklet from the insurance company as to their requirements and how-to tips.
- Duplicate pictures/tapes/disks and give to the estate executor or someone who will inherit.
- Call in a qualified appraiser and pay to evaluate and place values on items. Get the appraisal in writing.
- Use your basic knowledge of the values of your items to determine how extensive the appraisal should be. Some appraisers charge per item, while others charge per hour.

- The estate possessions register will be an indispensable tool in settling your estate with state and federal tax authorities.

- Normally a standard policy will cover personal possessions up to 60 percent of the amount of insurance on your home. For instance, a home insured for $100,000 will have $60,000 coverage on personal property. If the value of the antiques, collectibles, and fine art brings the total value of personal possessions above this percentage, additional coverage is recommended. This usually requires scheduling the items on the homeowners policy, meaning that each item is described, its value is listed, and a separate premium is paid.

APPENDIX H

REPRODUCTIONS

- The only defense against being taken in by fakes, fantasy items, reproductions, or copy cats is to be educated.
- Subscribe to *Antique & Collectors Reproduction News*, 408 Foster Drive, Des Moines, IA 50312-2514. 1-800-227-5531
- Study every book, journal, and newspaper about antiques that you can get your hands on. See Works Consulted for titles.
- Go to shops and malls to handle as much merchandise as possible.
- Go to museums to study their collections and books.
- Register for classes on antiques and collectibles.
- Ask questions.
- Don't be afraid to listen to those "gut" feelings about an item that just doesn't seem right to you.

Appendix I

PRONUNCIATION KEY

This pronunciation key is a little unorthodox in its approach. The words are divided into syllables, using familiar words rather than conventional phonetic standards. The stressed syllable is underlined. The easiest way to pronounce these often mispronounced words is to say them out loud several times using this simple method. The definitions are also simplified. I recommend further reading in a good dictionary or a compendium of collector terms, such as *A-Z of Collector's Terms,* by Therle Hughes, published by Bounty Books, 2001.

A

abalone (ab a <u>low</u> knee): large mollusk that is a source of mother-of-pearl

antimacassar (antee ma <u>cass</u> er): fabric or crochet work draped over an upholstered chairback to protect it from macassar oil, a nineteenth-century hair dressing

Armand Marseille (are <u>mon</u> mar <u>say</u>): (1880s–1920s). German doll manufacturer

art nouveau (art new <u>voe</u>): style from the late nineteenth, early twentieth centuries, using curvilinear motifs often derived from nature

Aubusson (<u>oh</u> beh sohn): from the town in France. An ornate rug constructed in a flat tapestry weave, often in pastel colors

B

Baccarat (<u>bah</u> caw rah): manufacturer of fine glass decorative objects

baguette (<u>bag</u> get): long, thin rectangular stone

baroque (bah <u>roke</u>): irregularly shaped pearls

basalt (beh <u>salt</u>): Josiah Wedgwood's fine, unglazed stoneware, usually black with a dull gloss

bebe (beh <u>beh</u>): doll that has properties of a young child and a shorter, fatter body than a lady doll

Biedermeier (<u>bee</u> dur my er): (1820s–1850s), Austro-German furniture with opulent carving

Boehm (beam): porcelain sculptures of birds and historical figures

C

cabochon (<u>cab</u> eh shawn): oval-shaped, unfaceted precious stone

cabriole (<u>cab</u> ree ol): leg with outcurving at the knee, tapering and incurving about the foot

cartouche (car <u>toosh</u>): decorative scroll or border executed with a pen or brush

chalcedony (<u>kal</u> sid oh knee): mineral mixture of quartz and opal with a watery luster

champlevé enamel (shan lee <u>vay</u>): enamel fused into hollowed or incised areas of a metal base

chatelaine (<u>shat</u> lane): a hooklike clasp or chain for holding keys, trinkets, scissors, etc., worn at the waist by women

chinoiserie (chin <u>wah</u> sir ee): European notions of Oriental designs

cliché (klee <u>shay</u>): electrotype duplicate of a woodcut or wood engraving

Clichy (clee <u>shee</u>): (established 1837), French manufacturer of paperweights

cloisonné (cloy zuh <u>nay</u>): enamelwork in which colored areas are separated by thin metal bands

D

Daguerreotype (da <u>ger</u> oh type): (1839) photographic process in which a picture made on a silver surface sensitized with iodine was developed by exposure to mercury vapors

decalcomania (dee <u>cal</u> coh <u>main</u> ee ah): (1860s) process of transferring pictures or designs from specially prepared paper onto furniture, metal, glass, or pottery

demi-parure (demi pa <u>roor</u>): part of a set of jewelry; two pieces

depose (dee <u>poze</u>): French for patent or copyright

Directoire (dee wreck <u>twar</u>): mid-1790s French furnishings using Greco-Roman forms and Egyptian motifs

E

eclectic (i <u>kleck</u> tick): made up of elements from different sources

ephemera (eh <u>fem</u> e rah): lasting a short time. Often paper collectibles are characterized as ephemera.

escutcheon (es <u>kutch</u> en): ornamental plate around a keyhole, door handle, drawer pull, etc.

etagere (a tah <u>zhar</u>): stand with a series of open shelves for displaying objects

F

Faberge, Peter Carl (fab er <u>zha</u>): (1846–1920) Russian goldsmith and jeweler

faience (fay <u>awns</u>): highly colored, tin-glazed earthenware or pottery

faux (foe): false

Favril (fav <u>reel</u>): Tiffany iridescent art glass

fraktur (<u>frock</u> tour): decorative watercolor and ink painting and calligraphy in Pennsylvania German tradition

funerary (<u>fyoo</u> neh rare ee): pertaining to funeral or burial

G

Gallé (gal <u>lay</u>): French; famous for cameo and cased glass wares

genre (<u>zhawn</u> reh): a class or category of artistic endeavor using a particular form, content, or technique

Givenchy (jviv <u>on</u> shee) French fashion house opened in 1952 specializing in clothing, accessories, perfumes, and cosmetics

Godey's (<u>go</u> dee): (1830) first women's magazine in the United States

Gouache (gwash): painting with opaque watercolors prepared with gum

H

Heisey (<u>high</u> see): (1893–1957) Ohio blown and molded glasswares

Hermès (air <u>meez</u>) French fashion house established in 1837 specializing in fine leather and silk goods and perfume

I

intaglio (in <u>tal</u> yo): incised carving with a figure or design beneath the surface

intarsia (in <u>tar</u> si a): decorative design of inlaid wood in a background of wood

J

jardiniere (jar din <u>air</u>): ornamental receptacle or stand holding plants or flowers

K

kaolin (<u>kay</u> oh lynn): China clay, degraded form of granite, one of the secrets of Chinese hard-paste porcelain; a white refractory clay

Kovel (ko <u>vel</u>): Ralph and Terry, expert collectors and authors of books on antiques

L

Lalique (lah <u>leak</u>): high quality French glass in art nouveau and art deco styles

lorgnette (lorn <u>yet</u>): pair of eyeglasses mounted on a handle

M

marquis (mar <u>key</u>): boat-shaped stone

Mauchline ware (mock <u>lean</u>): (1820s–1930s) small Scottish souvenir wood items with Tartan plaids and handpainted or pen-drawn scenes

Meissen (<u>my</u> sen): (c. 1708) porcelain factory near Dresden; made Europe's first hard-paste porcelain

N

netsuke (<u>net</u> ski, or, Japanese, net <u>tsoo</u> key): small figure in ivory, wood, metal, or ceramic, originally used as a buttonlike fixture on a man's sash from which small personal belongings were hung

Niloak (<u>nile</u> oak): an Arkansas pottery. Name derived from "kaolin" clay spelled backwards

Nippon (knee <u>pon</u>): a Japanese name for Japan

P

papier-mache (paper ma <u>shay</u>): paper pulp mixed with glue. Dries to a hard finish that can be drilled, sanded, or painted.

parure (pa <u>roor</u>): complete set of three or more pieces of matching jewelry

passementerie (pass <u>men</u> tree): trimming of braid, cord, or beads

philately (fill <u>lat</u> el ee): hobby of collecting stamps and other postal materials

petuntse (pi <u>tune</u> see): China stone, feldspar stone, one of the secrets of Chinese hard-paste porcelain

pique (peek <u>ay</u>): ornamentation by means of punched or stippled patterns, sometimes inlaid with metal, ivory, or tortoise shell

plique a jour (plea kah <u>zhoor</u>): enameling technique in which unbacked wirework is filled with transparent enamel resulting in a stained-glass effect

pontil (<u>pon</u> tul): iron rod used in glassmaking for handling the hot glass; also called punty; pontil mark

prie dieu (<u>pree</u> dyoo): a piece of furniture for kneeling on during prayer, having a rest above as for a book

provenance (<u>prov</u> en ance): place or source of origin, history and record of ownership

Q

Quezal (key <u>sal</u>): a Brooklyn, New York, art glass company created to rival Tiffany

Quimper (kam <u>pair</u>): pottery district in France, colorful tin-glazed pottery

R

repousse (ray pu <u>say</u>): hammering metal on the reverse side to create a relief design on the outside

RS Suhl (R. S. sewel): a province of Thuringia, Germany

S

Sabinot (sa <u>bee</u> no): opalescent glass figurines and animals

sgraffito/graffito (scra <u>feet</u> oh *or* gra <u>feet</u> oh): technique of scratching a design through an overglaze to reveal a different color underneath

Schlegelmilch (<u>schlay</u> gull milch): last name of makers of R.S., C.S., O.S., and E.S. porcelains

Schroeder (<u>schray</u> der): annual price guide

Sevres (sev): French porcelain made since 1756

Sotheby's (<u>suth</u> uh bees): famous auction house in New York and London

Steuben (stew <u>ben</u>): handmade, heavy lead crystal made by Steuben Glass Works, Corning, New York

T

Teco (<u>tea</u> ko): a line of art pottery by Terra Cotta Tile Works, Terra Cotta, Illinois

tete-a-tete (tate ah tate): head to head, between or for two persons only

Towle (toll): Massachusetts silver manufacturer

trompe l'oeil (<u>trohnp</u> lur y): trick of the eye; style of painting in which objects are photographically realistic

V

vermeil (ver <u>may</u>): copper, silver, or bronze, gilded with a thin layer of gold

vertigris (<u>vur</u> deh gres): green or blue patina that forms on copper, brass, or bronze when exposed to the atmosphere for a long time

vinaigrette (vin eh <u>gret</u>): small portable container with sponge scented with vinegar

W

wainscot (<u>wayne</u> scoat): paneled wood lining an interior wall

Winterthur (<u>win</u> ter tour): Henry Francis du Pont's Delaware estate that houses a world's premier collection of American decorative arts

Appendix J
FINDING AN ACCREDITED APPRAISER

Collectors, antiques dealers, estate managers, trustees, executors, attorneys, judges, bankers, investors, insurers, adjusters, and federal and state tax agencies may require the expertise and knowledge of a certified appraiser when a written opinion of value is needed. These documented valuations by a professional appraiser are drawn on prescribed methods of research, evaluation and report writing.

An appraiser may be needed for an estate settlement, insurance coverage or claims, bankruptcy, equitable distributions of property between heirs or in a marriage dissolution; civil or criminal legal proceedings, or for tax purposes.

The following are the organizations that are recognized in the appraisal industry as having accredited members who conduct antique and personal property appraisals. Their websites will provide you with how to find an appraiser in your local area, educational opportunities to become an appraiser, and conferences and seminars on the art of appraising.

American Society of Appraisers
800-272-8258
www.appraisers.org

International Society of Appraisers
312-224-2567
www.isa-appraisers.org

National Institute of Appraisers
800-676-2148
www.appraisersoffineart.com

WORKS CONSULTED

Listed below are specific articles and books consulted for this publication. In general, however, *Antique Trader Weekly* (antiquetrader.com) is the standard source of information for the industry and *Country Living Magazine* (countryliving.com) is always useful. A serious collector should subscribe to both. *Country Home Magazine* is also a good source to consult.

American Quilter's Society. *Protecting Your Quilts: A Guide for Quilt Owners*. Paducah, KY: American Quilter's Society, 1996.

Bennett, Jennifer. "Auction Arabesque." *Harrowsmith Country Life*, Oct. 1994.

Berthold-Bond, Annie. *Clean and Green: The Complete Guide to Nontoxic and Environmentally Safe Housekeeping*. Woodstock, NY: Ceres Press, 1994.

Chervenka, Mark. "How to Use an Eye Loupe." *Antique and Reproduction News*. March 1994.

Cloutier, Anne Marie. "Collecting U. S. Postage Stamps." *Country Living Magazine*. Jan. 2008.

Dart, Andrew. "The History of Postage Rates in the United States." *www.akdart.com/postrate.html*. Accessed December 2011.

Erlandson, Lisa. *www.lequilts.com/quilt_care*. Accessed December 2011.

Exposure's Guide to Preserving Your Family Memoirs. 1993. Write to 1 Memory Lane, Oshkosh, WI, 54903 for a copy.

Federal Emergency Management Agency, "Tips for the Care of Water-Damaged Family Heirlooms and Other Valuables," unpublished article.

Garrett, Charles L. *Successful Coin Hunting*. Dallas, TX: Ram Publishing, 1997.

"Gluing Furniture." *Martha Stewart Living Magazine*. March 1995.

Harrison, C. Robert. "Preserving Paper Collectibles." *Antique Trader Weekly*. Oct. 13, 1993.

Hays, Valorie. "Cleaning Your China," Flow Blue International Newsletter.

Herlocher, Dawn. Doll lecture. Institute of Antiques and Collectibles Summer Camp. Vera Cruz, PA. July 1995.

Hughes, Therle. *A-Z of Collector's Terms*. Secaucus, NJ: Bounty Books, 2001.

Japan Guide. *www.Japan-guide.com*. Accessed December 2011.

Jenkner, Carol. "Hooked Rugs of the Depression Era." *Antique Trader Weekly*. Oct. 21, 1992.

Johnson, Bruce E. "Advertising Art." *Country Living Magazine*. May 1995.

———. "American Pewter," *Country Living Magazine*. March 1994.

———. "Missing Parts." *Country Living Magazine*. Sept. 1988.

Kansas Historical Society. *www.kshs.org/p/preserverving-photographs-and-audio-visual-materials/12262*. Accessed December 2011.

Kovel, Ralph, and Terry Kovel. *Kovels' Know Your Antiques*. New York: Crown Trade Paperbacks, 1990.

Luscomb, Sally C. *The Collector's Encyclopedia of Buttons*. PA: Schiffer Publishing, 1992.

Mailand, Harold, F. *Consideration for the Care of Textiles and Costumes: A Handbook for the Non-Specialist*. Indianapolis, IN: Indianapolis Museum of Art, 1980.

Millhouse, Peggy. *Doll Clothes Cleaning and Restoring.* PA: Conestoga, 1996.

Minneapolis Institution of Arts. "The Arts of Asia History and Maps of Japanese Historical Periods," *www.artsmia.org/art-of-asia/history/chinese-dynasty-guide.cfm.* Accessed November 2011.

Moore, Alma Chesnut. *How to Clean Everything.* New York: Simon and Schuster, 1977.

Moorhouse, Judith. *Collecting Oriental Antiques.* NJ: Chartwell Books, 1990.

Ogden, Sherelyn. *Cleaning Books and Shelves.* Andover, MA: Northeast Document Conversation Center, 1999.

————. *Storage Methods and Handling Practices for Books.* Andover, MA: Northeast Document Conservation Center, 1999.

Orlofsky, Patsy. "The Collector's Guide for the Care of Quilts in the Home." In *The Quilt Digest 2,* 58–69. San Francisco: Kiracofe and Kile, 1984.

Phoenixmasonry Masonic Museum & Library. *PhoenixmasΔonry.org/masonicmuseum.* "Dating English Registry Marks." Accessed November, 2011.

Reader's Digest Practical Problem Solver. Pleasantville, NY: Reader's Digest Association, 1992.

Roeder, Mark A. "How to Sell Your Antiques and Collectibles." *Country Collectibles.* Fall 1994.

Scofield, Elizabeth, and Peggy Zalamea. *20th Century Linens and Lace.* PA: Schiffer, 1995.

Textile Museum. "Guidelines for the Care of Textiles." *www.textilemuseum.org/care.* Accessed December 2011.

Time-Life Books. "Care of Antique Rugs." *American Country.* Alexandria, VA: Time-Life Books, 1989.

———. "Caring for Glass." *American Country*. Alexandria, VA: Time-Life Books, 1989.

———. "Caring for Woodenware." *American Country*. Alexandria, VA: Time-Life Books, 1989.

U.S. Department of Agriculture. "Stain Removal from Fabrics: Home Methods." Farmers Bulletin #1474. Washington, DC, 1951.

U.S. Patent and Trademark Office website: USPTO Site Index, "Issue Year." *www.uspto.gov/patents/process/search/issueyear.isp*. Accessed Nov. 2011.

"Use the Right Glue to Make Things Stick." *Home Magazine*. July 1981.

Wikipedia. "History of United States Postage Rates." Accessed Nov. 2011.

Wikipedia. "History of the Internet." Accessed Nov. 2011.

Williams-Sonoma. "Guide to the Care of Cookware," Pamphlet. 1991.

Wright, Veva Penick. *Pamper Your Possessions*. MA: Barre Publishers, 1972.